BRUCE LEE 龍

IN MY OWN PROCESS

PRESENTED BY
THE FAMILY OF
BRUCE LEE

BRUCE LEE 龍

IN MY OWN PROCESS

GENESIS PUBLICATIONS
SINCE 1974

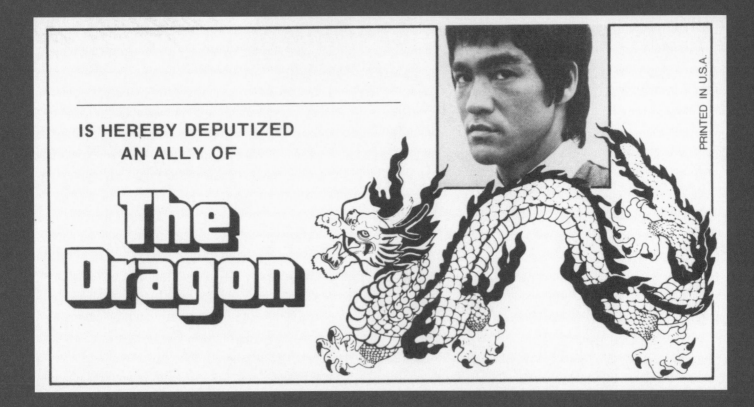

IS HEREBY DEPUTIZED
AN ALLY OF

The Dragon

PRINTED IN U.S.A.

genesis

genesis-publications.com

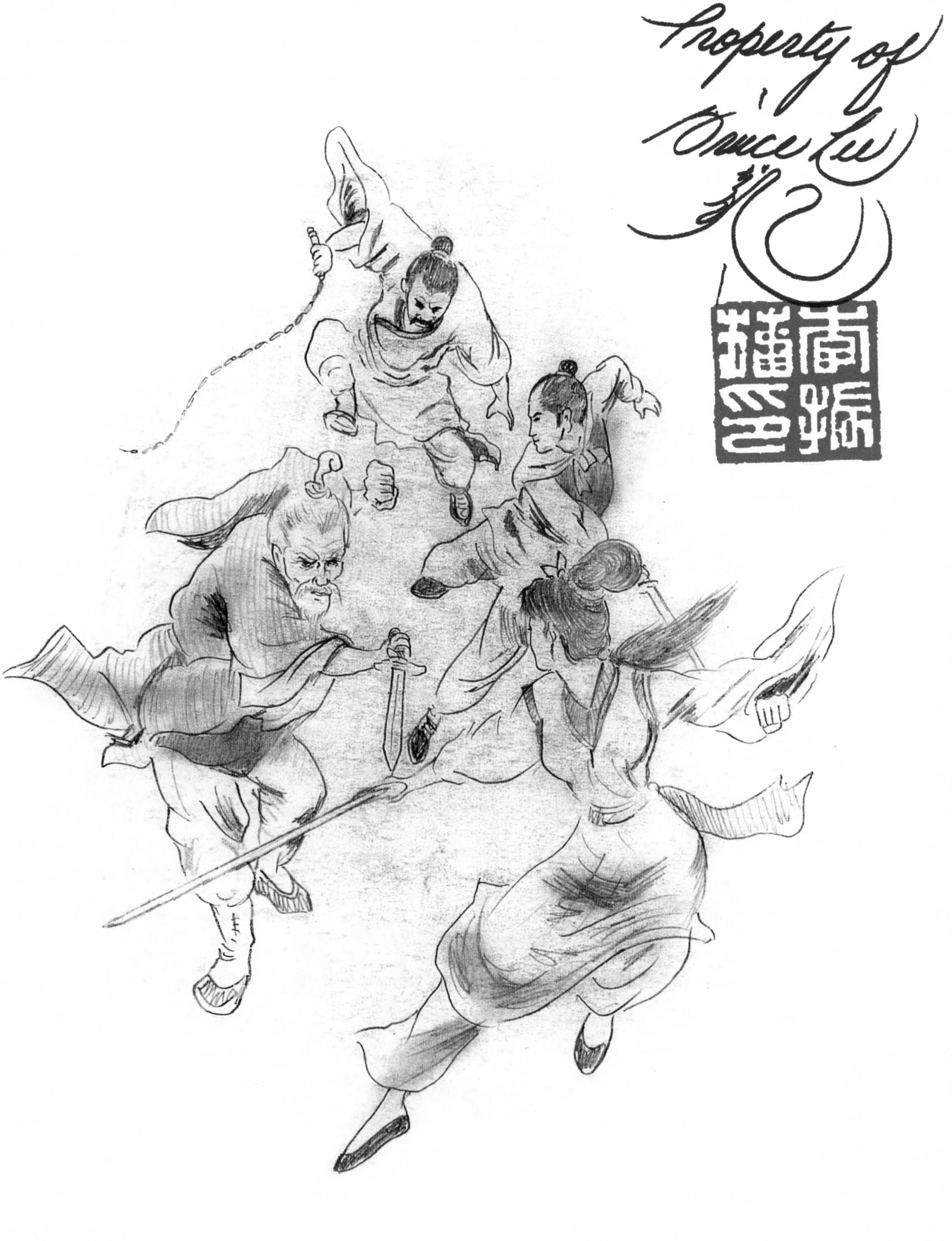
Property of
Bruce Lee

CONTENTS

JUN FAN GUNG FU INSTITUTE

振藩國術館

Using No Way As Way
Having No Limitation As Limitation

THE LEGEND OF GUNG FU
JACKIE CHAN

I will always cherish the days I had the privilege of working alongside Bruce Lee. At that time, I was relatively unknown, so the opportunity to collaborate with my idol was incredible. During the filming of *Fist of Fury* and *Enter the Dragon*, Bruce treated us, the stunt performers, with immense respect and patience. It was through his support and recognition that I was able to work on the set and earn welcome extra income through night shifts. To this day, whenever I watch these two movies, I proudly tell my friends that I was there.

By a stroke of luck, I encountered Bruce again on the streets of Hong Kong one day while on my way to go bowling. Much to my surprise, he asked if he could join me. Can you imagine how great that was? Escorting the world-renowned martial artist Bruce Lee to the bowling alley! When we got there, he mostly watched me play, deep in contemplation. And I acted as his personal bodyguard, shooing away photograph and autograph-hunters.

That turned out to be the last time I saw Bruce. Even today, the image of our parting remains vivid in my mind – as, dressed in a wide-collared shirt, bell-bottom trousers and light tan platform shoes, he bade me farewell with a wave of his hand.

On that day, I missed my chance to express my gratitude to him. So, seizing my opportunity now while contributing to this new book, I would like to solemnly say, Mr Bruce Lee, thank you.

Thank you for acquainting the world with Chinese martial arts. Thank you for showcasing the power of Chinese idols to global audiences, and thank you for inspiring countless generations of young martial arts enthusiasts. Furthermore, I am eternally grateful to you for acknowledging my work as a stunt performer all those years ago, offering me the chance to extend my presence on the set and enabling me to witness at first hand the essence of your talent.

Bruce Lee will forever be a shining light in the world of cinema and an idol in the hearts of fans worldwide. He was the spiritual leader of the martial arts movement and offered unwavering inspiration during our youth. His influence has been a tremendous positive force for countless individuals, and, for many others who faced challenges in their lives, he became an invaluable source of hope.

The legend of gung fu has found his new home in heaven. And the world will never know another Bruce Lee.

THE THINGS WE LEAVE BEHIND
KAREEM ABDUL-JABBAR

The other day I was driving home and I passed an estate sale. It was early morning and dozens of people were marching towards the house to pick over the small personal treasures accumulated over a lifetime. These are the things we leave behind, I thought, made valuable by our absence.

But there are other things we leave behind for which there is no price because their value cannot be measured. For most of us, the impact we had on our friends and family through a lifetime of love is the most important thing we leave behind. A few rare people also leave behind a legacy that reaches out far beyond their family and friends and enriches the lives of millions of people they have never even met.

Bruce Lee was one of those rare people.

Bruce was my teacher and friend, from the time I met him when I was a student at UCLA until his death five years later. I have told the story of our first meeting many times because, to me, it is the essence of who he was and the impact he had on others. Here's what happened at my first lesson:

Bruce asked his wife, Linda, to assist him in a demonstration. He told me to hold a thick training pad to my chest and instructed Linda to kick the pad. 'Bruce, I don't think this will work,' I said. 'I'm two feet taller and a hundred pounds heavier than Linda.' Bruce smiled but said nothing. 'Just hold it up to your chest,' Linda said. My chest was higher than her head so I lowered it a little. 'Your chest,' she said. 'Do you want Bruce to show you where that is?' 'OK, OK,' I said. I held it up to my chest, maybe even a few inches higher. 'Ready?' Bruce said. 'Ready,' I said, a little smugly. Bruce nodded at Linda. Suddenly, Linda fired off a kick that not only reached the pad, but the impact rocked me backward a few feet, readjusted my spine, and possibly rearranged the order of my teeth. They stood there smiling at the shocked expression on my face. 'OK,' I said, rubbing my chest. 'Teach me that.'

Let me unpack that lesson because what impressed me wasn't just the kick. Bruce could have easily done the demonstration himself, thereby proving to me, a much bigger man and a famous athlete, that he was my superior. Most teachers would have done that in order to establish their macho cred. He did not feel the need to do that. His lesson in his own humility had more impact on me than Linda's mighty kick. Yes, I wanted to be able to kick like Linda, but I also wanted to be as humble as Bruce.

Bruce's martial arts lessons had a big effect on how I played basketball. But Bruce and I talked about books and philosophy as much as we did about martial arts. He wasn't just teaching me a skill, he was teaching me a way of life.

I last saw Bruce 50 years ago, but his teachings helped shape the man I became and am always in the process of becoming. Miraculously, through his books and movies, he was able to have a similar impact on millions of others. That ability to positively affect so many people is one of the most precious things we can leave behind. And with books like the one you are now holding, his legacy will continue far into the future.

DISCIPLINE, PERSEVERANCE & PASSION
TONY HAWK

When I started skating it was fading from its first wave of semi-popularity, but I wasn't concerned about that. I just loved what it provided me in terms of my sense of self and my confidence. I was young enough to not think I was choosing a career. I just thought of it as an activity or a sport. But as I started to do it more often, I realised it spoke to me in a way that nothing else did.

Every time I skated, I learned a new technique. I didn't have much to gauge it on because I didn't have many peers that were skating. The only advanced skating I saw was in magazines and it seemed kind of out of reach to me because the skaters were older and bigger than me. So, I created my own style that fit with my size and strength, which was largely made fun of at the time. People called me a circus skater because they said I was doing these sort of baton twirls with my skateboard and they thought it wasn't hardcore or stylish. But it was my voice and I loved doing it. I just had to block out that negativity. I had to block out the insults because I just enjoyed it too much.

An ability and willingness to change direction is something that I associate with Bruce Lee. I'm not saying you should compromise what you do or stop following your passion; it's about fine-tuning it for your surroundings. It's about the perseverance and the discipline it takes just to keep it up, especially when there are no accolades for what you are doing.

Bruce Lee exemplified discipline and I've learned to carry that over into my personal life too. It's about becoming disciplined to act or practise in alignment with your values and with how you want to be. Eventually it becomes natural and the things that were initially difficult for you to become motivated to do become the only things you really want to do.

I landed my first 900 at the X Games. I didn't actually plan on trying it that night, because the event followed a 'best trick' format and I was relying on a trick that I had already done before called a varial 720. I did the trick pretty early on in the time allotted and so I had time to explore a new trick. The next trick on my list that I wanted to do was a 900. It was one of my life goals. So I started trying it more as an example for the crowd. Then as I started trying it, my spin and my speed were consistent and that had never happened before. I finally had this consistent approach and the attempts were getting closer and closer and so I realised that if I was ever going to make this, it was probably going to be in that moment. Well, I was either going to get really hurt or make it. Those were the only two endings I was going to accept. What people saw on that night was just a typical example of what it takes to learn a trick on a skateboard. That's the bottom line and I think that resonated with a lot of people. It is something that requires a lot of discipline, perseverance and passion.

I think the main parallel between Bruce Lee's philosophy and skating is the point about overcoming your perceived limits or the limits that others have somehow imposed on you. Bruce's character, his values, his ethos, are aspects that we still carry with us today. He demonstrated his unique qualities so memorably that his message still resonates and that is his legacy. When you say the name 'Bruce Lee', it's not just about a guy that does martial arts, it's a way of life.

INTRODUCTION SHANNON LEE

I have spent much of my time sharing my father's philosophies with the public, because, to me, they make up the foundation on which his life and legacy are built. The philosophies are also where my father's passions intersect with my own. But this is not a philosophy book. Surely, some of his philosophies are shared within these pages; they have to be to reflect the truth of the man. But this book is, above all, a beautifully compiled reflection on his life in images and words – and not only his own words, but others' as well.

That said, dear reader, I invite you to engage with this book through the lens of my father's philosophies nonetheless. But how would you do that if you are not familiar with Bruce Lee's philosophy and this is not a philosophy book? Well, I like to mention when discussing him that my father 'lived' his philosophies. He didn't just espouse them, he put them into practice. In fact, he liked to say that, if you are not careful, philosophy can become the disease for which it pretends to be the cure. (All talk and no walk!)

And so just what was Bruce Lee living? He lived the path of self-actualisation – to make one's soul real through physical and energetic expression. It could also be described as creating the very essence of yourself to such an intimate degree that it remains unique among humanity, or cultivating and expressing your talents, your mind, your body, your being to the level of creating something wholly your own, something unable to be copied by another human being at the signature level. I invite you to engage with these pages with that in mind and bear witness.

One thing about my father is that his energy is palpable within the images of him, both moving and still. And so I ask, can you sense it here? Can you sense the seed of this energy even within the boy and the young man? And what does it inspire in your imagination? Does it invite you to ask questions such as, what is the arc of skill? of excellence? of self-expression? Do you find a soul struggling to recognise itself here and was that soul successful?

And, more importantly, do you find a reflection of some aspect of yourself somewhere along Bruce Lee's journey? Are you an artist of life searching to reveal yourself? I have found that the beauty of my father's legacy often comes down to just that – that in him we see a reflection of some aspect of ourselves. We catch a glimpse of what is possible as a human being and thereby trigger some level of inspiration and invitation in the possibility we see. And yet, we also find just a man. Or a human being, as he liked to be thought of first and foremost.

And so after all the heady fare I have just spouted, I will also tell you this. Any invitation to engage with my father comes with a request to dive in and have fun. Play! Relate! Contemplate! Dream! Wonder! After all, Bruce Lee is just a finger pointing at the moon. He represents merely a direction taken. But the path is yours to follow towards the heaven you seek. May his personal artistry spur you on towards a deeper realisation of yourself!

Walk on!

1940-1958

早年時期 EARLY YEARS

一九四零年－一九五八年

In my own Process — by Bruce Lee

Any attempts to write a somewhat "meaningful" article — or else why write it at all — on how I, known as Bruce Lee by name, emotionally feel or how my instinctive reaction toward circumstance is no easy task. It all depends because it hold true yesterday might not be so to-day. In sure, I'm changing.

This article can very well be made less demanding should I indulge myself in the much practiced game of manipulating one's image. I am afraid My understanding as least can differentiate between self-actualization and self-image actualization. I know. I am not here to write any confession, but I am the type of man who takes responsibility to himself. Well, I chose to be honest. You are here.

To be a professional actor is the sum total of all that he is now spiritually, psychologically, physically, his experiences, his attitude, etc. etc. can go on and on. A true artist is one who can blend appropriately this oneness of commercial creativity and creative commerce. Such artist actor is known creatively as a deliverer and to the business men, he is a good risk off his box office. I have an automatic admiration toward film-makers who devote themselves to the "quality" of making an out of sight film. A film, because everyone of this unit is pouring his heart and soul in it, is what make this a success. — not just any one character.

BRUCE LEE
IN MY OWN PROCESS
LETTER ONE

What it boils down to is my sincere and honest revelation of a man called Bruce Lee. Just who is Bruce Lee? Where is he heading? What does he hope to discover? To do this a person has to stand on his own two feet and find out the cause of ignorance. For the lazy and hopeless, they can forget it and do what they like best.

Bruce Lee

Hong Kong

BRUCE LEE From boyhood to adolescence, I presented myself as a trouble-maker and was greatly disapproved of by my elders. I was extremely mischievous, aggressive, hot-tempered and fierce. Not only my 'opponents' of more or less my age stayed out of my way, but even the adults sometimes gave in to my temper. I never knew what it was that made me so pugnacious. The first thought that came into my mind whenever I met somebody I disliked was, 'Challenge him!' Challenge him with what? The only concrete thing that I could think of was my fists. I thought that victory meant beating down others, but I failed to realise that victory gained by the way of force was not real victory.

– *Newspaper article titled 'Me and Jeet Kune Do', 1972*

Above: Early photograph of Bruce in Hong Kong
Right: Bruce's birth certificate

GRACE HO Bruce was in movies from the age of six. He would play the rascal.

BRUCE LEE My father [Lee Hoi-chuen] was well acquainted with lots of movie stars and directors. Among whom there was the late Mr Chin Kam. They brought me into the studio and gave me some roles to play. I started off as a bit of a player and gradually became the star of the show.

– 'Me and Jeet Kune Do', 1972

GRACE HO My husband was an actor, comedian and opera star. In one of the films there was a part for a young boy who was supposed to be a bad influence, a fighter and uncontrollable. Bruce fit the role perfectly! The director helped him and Bruce was easy to direct because he was a natural.

Top left: Bruce's mother, Grace Ho, and father, Lee Hoi-chuen
Top right: Bruce in *Love Part II*, Hong Kong, 1955
Above left: Bruce (left) with his cousin, Frank (middle), and his brother, Peter (right)
Above right: Bruce with co-star Yee Chau-sui in *The Kid*, Hong Kong, 1950

GRACE HO Bruce was naughty like most boys his age but he really looked after his sisters. He loved to fight but mainly to keep fit.

An Orphan's Tragedy, **1955**
Bruce on set in *An Orphan's Tragedy*, Hong Kong, 1955, including (top left) with director Kei Chu and co-star Josephine Sia Fong-fong and (above left) with co-star Siuyi Yung

ST. FRANCIS XAVIER'S COLLEGE No. 27

Name........Bruce Lai Jun Fan........ Name in Chinese....李鎮藩

Address....9/F Nathan Road, 1st floor....

Date of Birth....27 Nov., 1941.... Identity Card No...178 5335

Schools attended....10 Sept., 1956 La Salle College 18 JUL 1959

Date of admission...10 Sept., 1956....Date of leaving school

General Appreciation...Poor student....

Religion....

Place and Date of Baptism....

Place and Date of 1st Communion....

Place and Date of Confirmation....

Remarks....West G.H.S. June 1955

ST. FRANCIS XAVIER'S COLLEGE

KOWLOON

九龍聖芳濟書院

Name....Bruce Lee....

Class/Form....IV B....

Subject....Dictation....

LINDA LEE CADWELL He started learning English in Hong Kong when he was 12. In his first English class, the teacher told everybody to write down their English name and he did not know his name was Bruce so he looked on the next kid's paper and wrote that name – 'John'. Nobody called him Bruce at that time.

GRACE HO [Bruce] was educated at La Salle College and then St Francis Xavier's College until he was 18, when I thought it was time for him to return to the States to further his studies.

Top: High school identification card
Above left: Bruce in Hong Kong
Above right: School dictation notebook

GRACE HO He started learning martial arts at the age of 13 with Yip Man, his Chinese instructor.

ROBERT LEE Bruce grew up as a bit of a mischievous kid, he was always involved in fights. One day he and his buddy were in a restaurant and after the meal they came out and they were surrounded by a rival gang and they got into a fight. Luckily at that time we had a car at home and, when the gang saw the car approaching, they fled. That more or less saved Bruce. After that he felt like he should protect himself in a better way. At the time wing chun was the in thing. It was a system of martial arts, of Chinese gung fu, that believes in economy and straight punches and things like that. To him that was the most logical approach to protection. So he decided to talk to this old gentleman by the name of Yip Man.

NORA MIAO In Hong Kong martial arts is something you grow up with. Fathers, brothers, friends and cousins in one way or another are involved with bettering themselves physically and mentally. The Chinese way of doing this is through martial arts and the philosophies behind them.

Above left and opposite: Bruce with Yip Man,
Hong Kong, 1963
Above right: Bruce with his brother Robert,
Hong Kong, 1963

BRUCE LEE You can well say that I do not have any style, though I have to admit that I initiate from my wing chun instructor, Mr Yip Man. We had tea not too long ago, and, although our ideas differ, I respect this instructor of mine. Whatever happens, he is my wing chun instructor.

– *In My Own Process, Letter One*

少林詠春派掌門

葉問老師

Professor Yip Man
        leader of the Wing Chung School

The last Master of the Wing Chung school
was Professor Yip, borned in Fut San
in Southern China. Professor Yip
started a study of the various schools
of Gung Fu at the age of 8, till
he met Professor Chan Wa Shun,
and immediately devoted his full
energies to his art, the Wing Chung
School. Now he is the present
leader of that school. Professor Yip
is truely a Gung Fu great, and
is respected by the other instructors
of various schools. He is famous
for his "sticking hand", in which
he attaches his hand to the
opponent and subdues him WITH
HIS EYES SHUT! At the age of
60 he is still active, and none
of his students can even
touch him.

SHANNON LEE Yip Man would always teach using Chinese wisdom, whether it was Taoism, such as talking about the bamboo versus the oak tree, or yin and yang. The teaching was very much about when to yield and when to be forceful, which I know must have been difficult for a young man who wanted to get out there and win.

JEFF CHANG There are parallels between kung fu movies and hip hop. When Bruce starts learning wing chun in Hong Kong, street fighting culture had taken hold and different schools had set up shop. They would challenge each other, which of course is the basic plot of every kung fu film. But it was an underground culture. The British had literally outlawed it.

Likewise in hip hop, you had these underground music cultures and it's about competition to see who's better. It's all about the battle. Battling in hip hop is the key to stylistic dominance. In kung fu it's all about which style is better. At the root of it is young people trying to figure out how to live with each other and there's this desire for competition and fun.

It was also about rebellion. In Hong Kong they tried to ban street fights. The British colonial administration was afraid these youths would turn from fighting each other to fighting them. The same thing happened with hip hop. They banned people from carrying boom boxes around, from gathering, and they instituted curfews. It was all about youth rebellion and to the authorities that was dangerous.

TAKY KIMURA When he was in Hong Kong I think he felt that the wing chun system was probably the most realistic in terms of economy of motion and minimising the classicalness of things. He always went by the axiom that the most simple and direct action was the most realistic. He likened it to swimming on dry land to swimming in the water. He said, 'At some point in time if you continue to swim on dry land, you've got to get into the action and swim in the water.'

Bruce in Hong Kong
Opposite: Page from Bruce's scrapbook

SHANNON LEE My father had been in approximately 20 films by the age of 18. His father was an actor in the Chinese opera who toured the US with his wife in 1940, which is how my father came to be born in San Francisco. My father's most notable childhood performance was probably his starring role in *The Orphan*, which was the last film he did before leaving Hong Kong to live in the US. The film was submitted to the Venice Film Festival back in 1959 and was then lost for 30 years until it was discovered still in storage in Venice and returned to the Hong Kong Film Archive.

This page and opposite: Bruce in *The Orphan*,
Hong Kong, released 3 March 1960

MON.	TUES.	WED.	THURS.	FRI.	SAT.
7:00 5:30	7:00 - 9:00	7:00 - 9:00	7:00 - 9:00	7:00 - 9:00	7:00 - 9:00
8:00 - 9:00	a). STOMACH	a). STOMACH	a). STOMACH	a). STOMACH	a). STOMACH
a). STOMACH	b). FLEXIBILITY	b). FLEXIBILITY	b). FLEXIBILITY	b). FLEXIBILITY	b). FLEXIBILITY
b). FLEXIBILITY	c). CYCLING	c). RUN.	c). CYCLING.	c). RUN.	c). CYCLING.
c). RUN					
12 — 1	11:00 - 12:00	12 - 1	11:00 - 12:00	12 12:00	11:00 - 12:00
RUN	WEIGHT TRAINING.	RUN	WEIGHT TRAINING	RUN	WEIGHT TRAINING
5:30 - 6:30	5:30 - 6:30	5:30 - 6:30	5:30 - 6:30	5:30 - 6:30	5:30 - 6:30
PUNCHING.	KICKING.	PUNCHING.	KICKING.	PUNCHING.	KICKING.

SECRET

SECRET

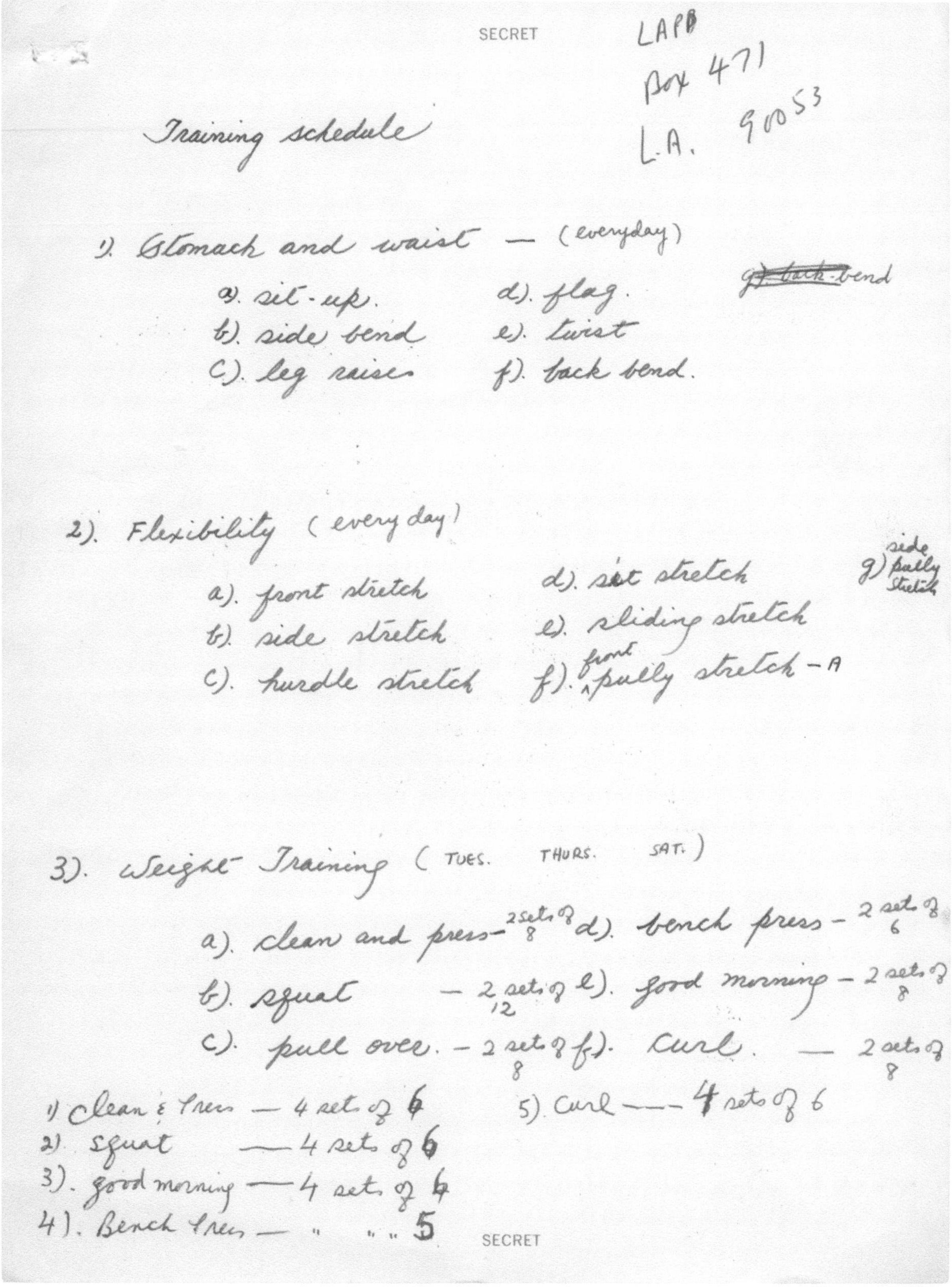

LAPD
Box 471
L.A. 90053

Training schedule

1). Stomach and waist — (everyday)

    a). sit-up.   d). flag.   ~~g). back bend~~

    b). side bend   e). twist

    c). leg raise   f). back bend.

2). Flexibility (every day)

    a). front stretch   d). sit stretch   g) side pully stretch

    b). side stretch   e). sliding stretch

    c). hurdle stretch   f). front pully stretch — A

3). Weight Training (TUES. THURS. SAT.)

    a). clean and press — 2 sets of 8   d). bench press — 2 sets of 6

    b). squat   — 2 sets of 12   e). good morning — 2 sets of 8

    c). pull over. — 2 set of 8   f). curl.   — 2 sets of 8

1) clean & press — 4 sets of 6   5) curl — 4 sets of 6

2). squat   — 4 sets of 6

3). good morning — 4 sets of 6

4). Bench Press — " " 5

This page and opposite: Training schedule. Throughout his life Bruce adapted and perfected his training schedules. The one featured here was written in 1967 during his time in the US

SEATTLE 西雅圖

1959-1966

一九五九年二一九六六年

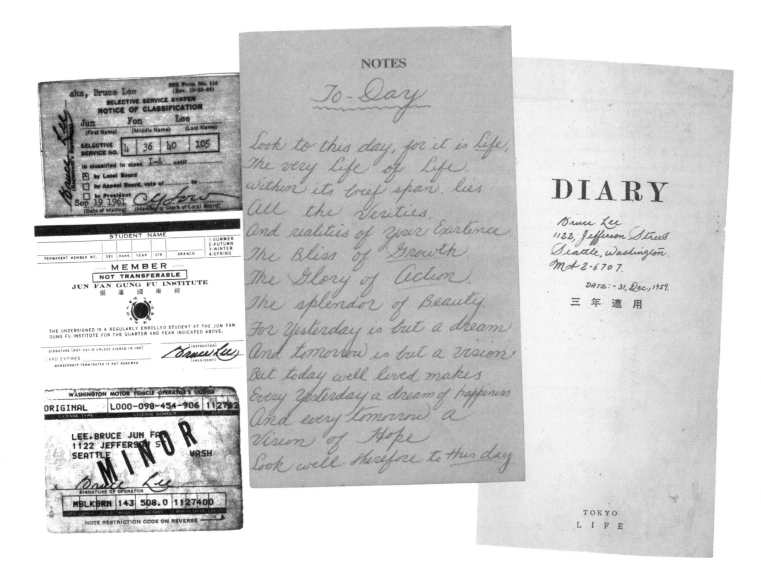

NOTES

To-Day

Look to this day, for it is Life,
The very Life of Life.
Within its brief span lies
All the Verities,
And realities of your Existence
The Bliss of Growth
The Glory of Action.
The splendor of Beauty.
For Yesterday is but a dream
And tomorrow is but a vision
But today well lived makes
Every Yesterday a dream of happiness
And every tomorrow a
Vision of Hope
Look well therefore to this day

DIARY

Bruce Lee
1122, Jefferson Street
Seattle, Washington.
MA 2-6707.

DATE: - 31, Dec., 1959.
三 年 連 用

TOKYO
LIFE

BRUCE LEE
IN MY OWN PROCESS
LETTER FIVE

Though we possess a pair of eyes, most of us do not
really see in the true sense of the word. True seeing, in
the sense of choiceless awareness, leads to new discovery,
and discovery is one of the means to uncovering our
potentiality. However, when this same pair of eyes is used
to observe or discover other people's faults we are quick
with ready-made condemnation. For it is easy to criticise
and break down the spirit of others, but to know yourself
takes maybe a lifetime.

Left: Bruce's Selective Service draft card,
dated 19 September 1961, membership card
to the Jun Fan Gung Fu Institute, Seattle, and
Washington state driver's licence, minor
age designation

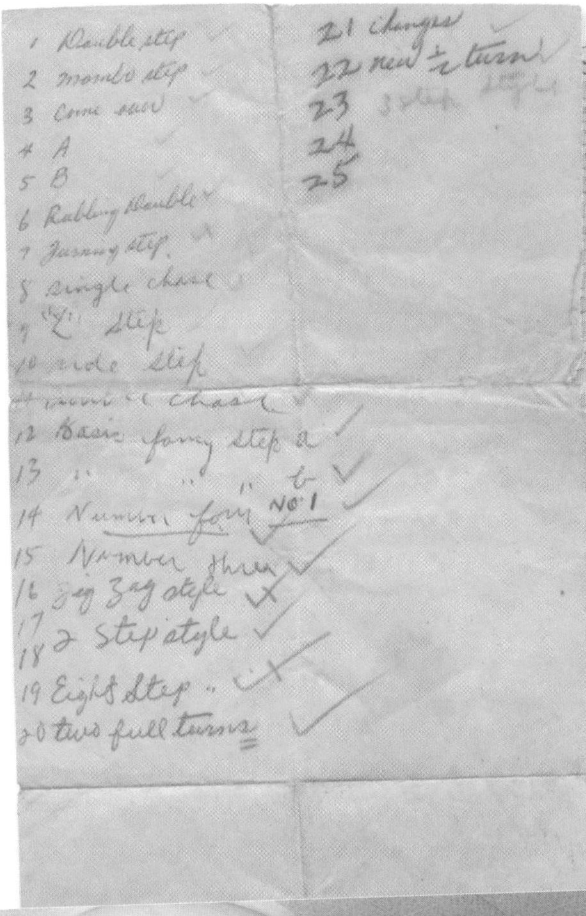

Left handwritten note:

1 double step
2 mambo step
3 come over
4 A
5 B
6 Rolling double
7 fancy step
8 single chase
9 "L" step
10 side step
11 double chase
12 Basic fancy step a
13 " " " b
14 Number four NO 1
15 Number three
16 Zig Zag style
17 2 step style
18 2 step style
19 Eight step "
20 two full turns

21 changes
22 new ½ turn
23 3 step 2 step
24
25

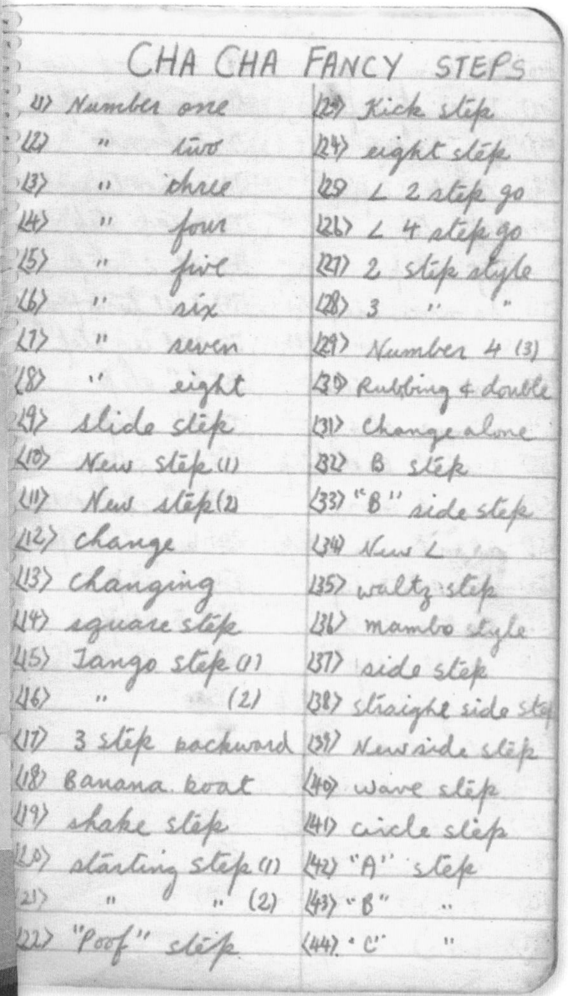

Notebook page — CHA CHA FANCY STEPS:

(1) Number one	(23) Kick step
(2) " two	(24) eight step
(3) " three	(25) L 2 step go
(4) " four	(26) L 4 step go
(5) " five	(27) 2 step style
(6) " six	(28) 3 " "
(7) " seven	(29) Number 4 (3)
(8) " eight	(30) Rolling & double
(9) slide step	(31) change alone
(10) New step (1)	(32) B step
(11) New step (2)	(33) "B" side step
(12) change	(34) New L
(13) changing	(35) waltz step
(14) square step	(36) mambo style
(15) Tango step (1)	(37) side step
(16) " (2)	(38) straight side step
(17) 3 step backward	(39) New side step
(18) Banana boat	(40) wave step
(19) shake step	(41) circle step
(20) starting step (1)	(42) "A" step
(21) " " (2)	(43) "B" "
(22) "Poof" step	(44) "C" "

LINDA LEE CADWELL When he left Hong Kong at 18 and his parents put him on the boat to come over to San Francisco, they gave him $100. He was in steerage, in third class, in the boat and where did he end up by the time he got to San Francisco? Up in first class, teaching people dancing! That was a gift that he had; he knew how to dance. He was cha-cha champion of Hong Kong. So, he figured how to get up to the top of the boat. That's how he got started in San Francisco too, by teaching dancing. He was teaching Bob Lee and his wife. Bob Lee was the brother of James Lee, the gung fu man that he eventually became partners with. He was very good at making connections. And, of course, he was very personable.

ROBERT LEE Bruce learned cha-cha from a Filipino musician. Back then it was very popular to go to dance halls, so he would go with different girls and it was there that he met his cha-cha teacher. Bruce with his good personality talked to this guy and said that he could probably show him some martial arts moves but he would have to show him some cha-cha steps in return. That's how he learned it.

Then, some time later, there was a poster about a dance contest with prizes and so forth and Bruce thought it would be a great way to show people how good a dancer he was. But he wasn't sure who to bring as a partner. If he picked one of the girls he was dating the others would get jealous and he didn't want that, so he decided to teach me instead. Nobody could say anything if he brought his brother! We joined and we came first place. It was so much fun.

Opposite and above left: Bruce teaching cha-cha on the ship to San Francisco
Right: Bruce with his brother Robert at a cha-cha competition, Hong Kong

IHK+ 5 5/16"

22A

Think of a fly
Think of a flea
When you do the cha cha
You'll think of me.

29, April, 1959 (Wednesday) left
Hong Kong at night 10 P. M.

17, May, 1959 (Sunday) arrived
in San Francisco

SHANNON LEE My father didn't stay in San Francisco for long – the plan was always to continue on to Seattle. While he was in San Francisco initially, he taught dance lessons and that was how he met some of his friends from the Bay Area like George Lee and Allen Joe. George made a lot of workout equipment for my father, and, later, it was Allen who got him into bodybuilding. This is an important part of the story because it was George Lee who introduced my father to James Lee. James Lee was the reason my father moved to Oakland – to open his second gung fu school with James. So, although my father wasn't in San Francisco for long, it was an important stop along the way. He met great people that ended up being lifelong friends.

Top: Bruce shortly after his arrival in
San Francisco, 1959

Top: Bruce and Peter Wong outside University of Washington, where Bruce studied philosophy
Above: Near Ruby Chow's restaurant, which was owned by a family friend. Bruce rented a room here

JEFF CHANG Moving to Seattle was a shock. Suddenly he was working in a restaurant, washing dishes and dealing with wealthy white customers who treated him like a Chinaman. Those experiences created within him a rage for justice and a deep feeling of empathy for the underdog. I think that's the spirit you see him carry through his movies, that depth of feeling for people who are struggling. Seattle is where it all begins.

LINDA LEE CADWELL He would buy books of American idioms so that he would not sound like a fresh-off-the-boat guy. He learned very quickly. Sometimes he would say funny things and I would go, 'What?' Some of those books were written strangely. He always had a slight English accent. I used to stand in front of him and I would say, 'OK, I want you to say "sport".' And he would say, 'Spoht'. They taught the Queen's English in Hong Kong. He was so good at writing English that when we were in college together and I had to write an essay about *Animal Farm* for my English class he wrote the essay for me and I got an A grade for it. His grammar was so good, better than most of us native speakers. However, you can see in his later writings that when he was following a train of thought he would often make a mistake with the grammar because he was thinking in Chinese. But if he wanted to produce a finished document his English was perfect.

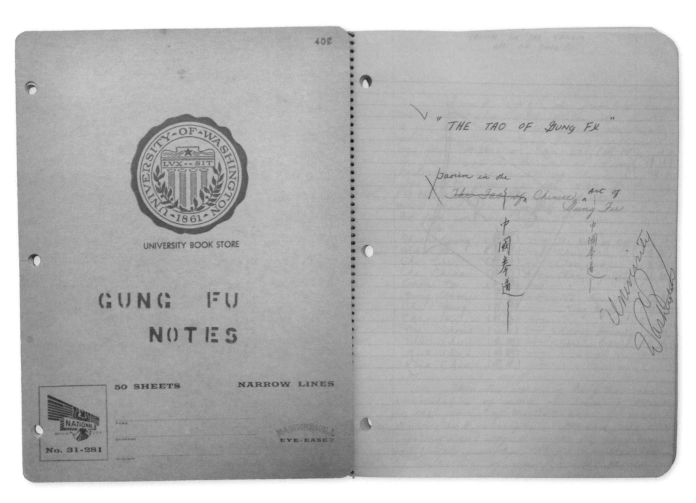

BRUCE LEE One part of my life is gung fu. This art has been a great influence in the formation of my character and ideas. I practise gung fu as a physical culture, a form of mental training, a method of self-defence and a way of life. Gung fu is the best of all martial arts; yet the Chinese derivatives of judo and karate, which are only basics of gung fu, are flourishing all over the United States. This so happens because no one had [yet] heard of this supreme art; also there are no competent instructors. I believe my long years of practice back up my title to become the first instructor of this movement. There are yet long years ahead of me to polish my techniques and character. My aim, therefore, is to establish the first gung fu institute that will later spread out all over the United States (I have set a time limit of ten to fifteen years to complete the whole project).

Gung fu, the centre of the oriental arts of self-defence, is a philosophical art that serves to promote health, to cultivate the mind, and to provide a most efficient means of self-protection. Its philosophy is based on the integral parts of the philosophies of Taoism and Chan (Zen) – the ideal of being harmonious with and not against the force of the opponent. Just as a butcher preserves his knife by cutting along the bones, a gung fu man preserves himself by complementing the movements of the opponent.

The word gung fu means 'discipline' and 'training' towards the ultimate reality of the object – be it health promotion, mind cultivation or self-protection. There is no distinction to make between the opponent and the self because the opponent is but the complementary part. There is no conquering, struggling, or dominating, and the idea is to 'fit' harmoniously your movement into that of the opponent. When he expands, you contract; when he contracts, you expand. Expansion then is interdependent with contraction and vice versa, each being the cause and result of the other.

– Essay on gung fu, untitled

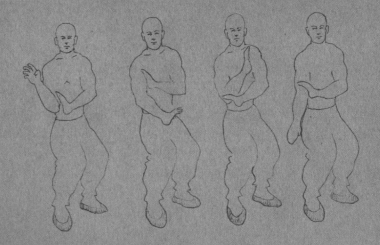

GUNG FU

TITLE: "THE TAO OF GUNG FU"

CONTENTS

Introduced by...............

CHINESE GUNG FU

Philosophical Art of Self Defense

Private Lessons
Group Lessons
Class Lessons   Phone

← 30B   3 1/2 11   →

ht: Bruce breaking bricks in his room

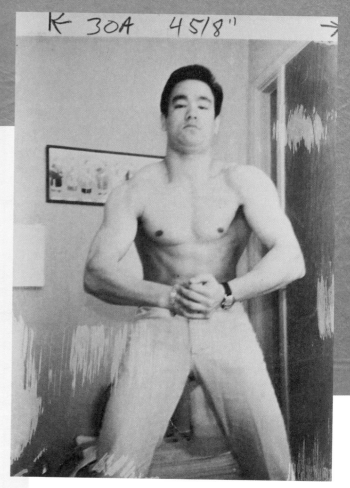

Bruce Lee's Way Of Gung Fu

K 30A 45/8"

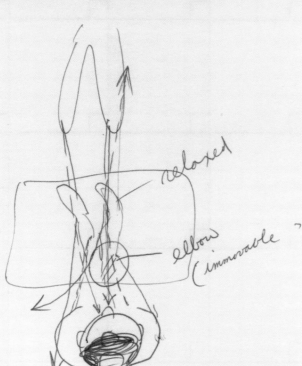

relaxed

elbow (immovable)

Top left: Gung fu demonstration with friend and
student Taky Kimura, Seattle
Top right: Bruce's notebook
Above: Bruce in his room at Ruby Chow's
Left: Sketch of fighting practice

GROUP 1

THE BASIC BLOWS :— (a) STRAIGHT RIGHT (HIGH & LOW) — LONG
AND SHORT RANGE
(b) STRAIGHT LEFT (HIGH & LOW) — LONG
AND SHORT RANGE
(c) GLIDING SLANT PUNCH
(d) BACK FIST
(e) THE HOOK.
(ALL THE ABOVE WITH FOOTWORK.)

GROUP 2

THE BASIC KICKS :—(a) STRAIGHT KICK (MEDIUM & LOW)
(b) SIDE KICK (MEDIUM & LOW)
(c) TOE KICK (STRAIGHT & HOOK)
(d) ROUND HOUSE ~~KICK~~ & HIGH KICK
(FOR PRACTICE ONLY)
(ALL THE ABOVE WITH FOOTWORK)

GROUP 3

BASIC DEFENSE :—(a) THE FINGER STOP STRIKE
(b) THE HIGH GUARD & STRIKE
(c) THE LOW GUARD & STRIKE
(d) THE INSIDE PARRY & STRIKE
(e) THE LOW PARRY & STRIKE
(f) THE MOVING OUT OF LINE & STRIKE
(g) THE SWALLOWING IN & STRIKE
(h) THE SIDE STEP STRIKE

GROUP 4

BASIC FOOTWORK ;— (a) ADVANCING   (b) RETREATING
(c) CIRCLING RIGHT (d) CIRCLING LEFT

GROUP 5

CLASSICAL TECHNIQUES ;—(a) SLAPPING HAND STRIKE
(b) HOOK JERK* STRIKE (SINGLE & DOUBLE
(c) THE BACK FIST STRIKE (LEFT & RIGH

BRUCE LEE My reason in doing this is not the sole objective of making
money. The motives are many and among them are: I like to let the
world know about the greatness of this Chinese art; I enjoy teaching
and helping people; I would like to have a well-to-do home for my
family; I like to originate something; and the last but yet one of the
most important is because gung fu is part of myself.

– Letter to Pearl Tso, September 1962

Bruce teaching gung fu at home. Bruce's first
student, Jesse Glover, is featured (bottom photo),
Seattle, December 1960

W. KAMAU BELL I can't imagine the pressure that Bruce was under when he decided to teach non-Chinese students. He had to trust the thing inside of him that told him to do things his way but he knew that that was going to make things harder.

KAREEM ABDUL-JABBAR It is so important for us to understand community. Too many people care about what you look like or what your culture is. As Dr King said, it's all about your innate quality. That's what it's all about. That's why Bruce never said, 'Well I'm only going to ever teach Chinese people.' He was going to teach everybody that had a good heart and had the discipline to learn this and respect it. That's what he was about.

Top: Bruce's grade summary from the University of Washington
Above left: Bruce with Ed Parker, founder of American Kenpo Karate
Above right: Bruce in Shatin, Hong Kong, 1963

RUBY CHOW'S
1122 JEFFERSON STREET
SEATTLE 4, WASHINGTON
MA. 2-6707

Mr. BRUCE LEE
1122 Jefferson Street
Seattle, Washington

This is your
CHECK ROOM TICKET

❧

The fat man on the
reverse side of this
ticket is the Chinese

GOD OF HAPPINESS

We sincerely hope he will
watch over you, and your
visit at Ruby Chow's will
be a joyous one.

(This ticket MUST be surrender-
ed for the return of checked items.
If you would like an extra ticket as
a souvenir, please ask the girl at
the check room.)

RUBY CHOW'S

Broadway at Jefferson
Seattle 4, Washington
MAin 2-6707

JESSE GLOVER I was fortunate enough to become Bruce Lee's
first student. I first saw Bruce as he came out from Ruby
Chow's, crossed over the street and headed down
Broadway. One day I walked up to him and asked him
if he was Bruce Lee and if he did gung fu and he said yes.
I asked him if he'd teach me and he said yes. And that
was the beginning.

Bruce outside Ruby Chow's, Seattle,
December 1960

2月 6日

19 SUN. 曜日 天候

To-day at around 12:30 took
Yeung, Jesse and I went down
to the YMCA where we met
Kimura (2nd dan black belt) All
of them are impressed by my
Gung Fu and ask me to teach
them.

From the left.
Jesse Glover, Judo Champion
of the Pacific Northwest
Bruce Lee.
Howard Hall, Judo and
boxing practioner.
Pat Hooks, 2nd degree
black belt holder
of the Kodokan.

Top: Gung fu demonstration with Jesse Glover
at a trade fair in Seattle, 1961
Left: Bruce with his students Jesse Glover,
Howard Hall and Pat Hooks

DOUG PALMER I first saw Bruce when he gave a demo at a street fair in Seattle's Chinatown during the summer of 1961. I had just finished my junior year in high school.

When Bruce stood up there on the stage in his black gung fu uniform, he didn't seem all that impressive at first. He looked rather slender, smaller than a high school running back, not even a welterweight. The three students who assisted in the demonstration, one black, one white, one Asian, were all older and more imposing physically. But once Bruce moved, he commanded the stage. I was impressed by the demo and asked around to see if I could wangle an introduction. When he moved that first time I saw him, he exploded. His hands were just a blur; the power in his snapping fists was palpable as he missed his students' noses by millimetres. I was blown away.

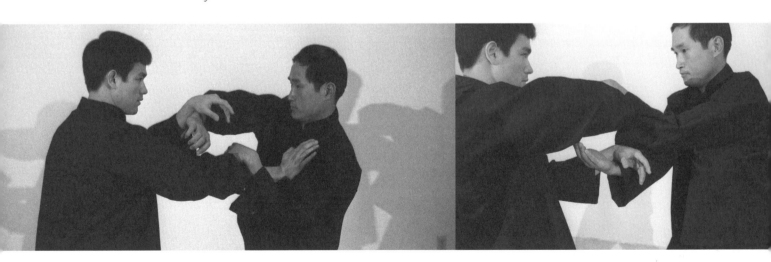

Top left: Bruce with Doug Palmer and friend, Hong Kong, 1963
Top right: Bruce and Doug with Eunice Lam, who would later marry Bruce's elder brother Peter
Above: Bruce and Ted Wong demonstrating chi sao

DOUG PALMER Two other aspects of the demonstration also made an impression. One was the exotic grace of a praying mantis form he executed, which was quite unlike anything I had ever seen before. The second thing that stuck with me was the demonstration of chi sau, the 'sticking hand'. Once he closed with his opponent and their wrists came in contact, he deflected all attempted blows and launched counterattacks with his eyes closed. I had never seen anything like that either.

A week or so later I was at another street fair called Bon Odori, featuring Japanese folk dances in front of what was then the main Buddhist temple.

Towards the end of the evening, I felt a tap on my shoulder. I stopped and turned around. A young Asian man stood there, a pace or two away. The circulating crowd parted and flowed around us. He leaned slightly back from the waist, his eyes hooded, a neutral expression on his face. 'I heard you were looking for me', he said.

I realised it was Bruce Lee. Facing him, I was initially nonplussed. On an unconscious level, I understood that his stance, although unmenacing and not overtly martial in appearance, was one from which he was prepared to react to whatever I did. Later, I realised it was a variation of the way he taught us to stand if faced by a potentially threatening situation. It gave the appearance of alertness without concern, confidence and readiness without aggressive intent.

I stuck out my hand and introduced myself. I told him that I had seen his recent demonstration in Chinatown, and was interested in taking lessons. He thought it over, then shrugged noncommittally and told me when they practised.

'Drop by sometime, check it out,' he said. 'If you're still interested, we'll see.'

He melted back into the crowd. I had no idea where they practised, or how I was going to get there. But I knew I'd find a way to show up.

Top: Bruce practising with Jesse Glover
Middle: Bruce, blindfolded, in wing chun demo with Dan Lee for a 1967 issue of *Black Belt*
Bottom: Bruce and Doug Palmer, Hong Kong, 1963

武 术

Deflection

The word "Gung Fu" includes
techniques of hands, feet, knees,
elbows, shoulders, head, and thighs;
the thirty-six throws; the seventy
two joint locks, and the eighteen
different weapons.

Swordplay is the most difficult
of all arts in Gung Fu. It
requires at least 10 years of
hard training to be a master of
it. The sword must be united with
the mind, and be used as the
limb of the body.

Wrist Thrust

钩 柳葉刀 雁翅刀 戒刀 斬馬刀 朴刀（滾風刀） 劍

敗中取勝左

鐺

矛

戟

棍

單刀式
(Single Sword)

蹬腿后瓦槍
(Spear play

雙刀式

Two swordplay

三節棍

Three section chain
stick (Staff)

虛步肩背棍
(Stick play
(staff)

騰空提膝下截刀

大刀對棍
Big Sword against Stick

Bruce's scrapbook

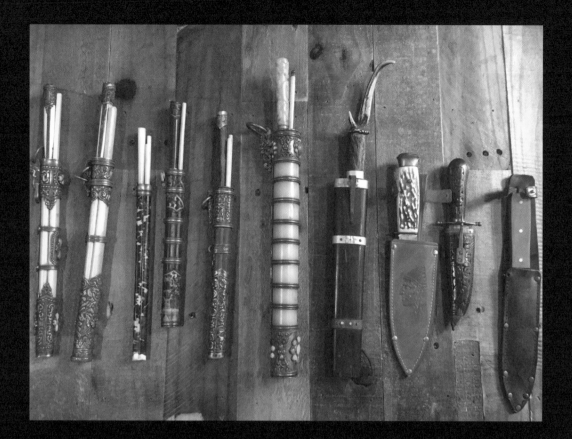

DOUG PALMER I had friends who practised judo and I had heard of karate, but I had never heard of gung fu before seeing Bruce's demo. I was unaware that it had a long history in China, or that it was taught within Chinese communities across the US. Having boxed since fifth grade, I appreciated the moves Bruce made with his hands but the legs added a whole new dimension. The need to defend against kicks to the shin, knee or groin, or higher, signalled what seemed to me at the time to be a total fighting system.

BRUCE LEE Gung fu originated in China. It is the ancestor of karate and jujitsu. It's more of a complete system and more fluid. By that I mean there is more flow and continuity instead of one movement, two movements and then stop. The best example is a glass of water. Why? Because water is the softest substance in the world yet it can penetrate the hardest rock. Water is also insubstantial. By that I mean you cannot grasp hold of it. You cannot punch it and hurt it, so every gung fu man is trying to do that. Be soft like water, and flexible. Adapt yourself to the opponent.

– Screen test for The Green Hornet, 1965

MOZEZ One of Bruce's key quotes, 'Be like water', reveals a thinking that I try to identify with and apply to my life. The importance of knowing when to be calm and when to be powerful. We all need to become like water.

be like WATER making its way through cracks.

Nothingness cannot be confined,
The softest thing cannot be snapped

A selection of knives and daggers belonging to Bruce

JEFF CHANG Bruce was born in San Francisco but it's only really with his return to the US in 1959 that he starts to become an Asian American. I say 'Asian American' specifically because he immediately becomes very aware of his minority status. He's forced to live in Chinatown – a segregated neighbourhood in San Francisco and then he moves to Seattle, which at the time was 95 percent white. He was living in the Central District where you had black people, Chinese, Japanese, Filipinos, Native Americans, Latinos and some whites. Bruce had grown up in a majority Chinese culture in Hong Kong – albeit under a form of apartheid in which the British were running the colony – but that gave him the tools to be able to relate to people like Jesse Glover and Taky Kimura and the disenfranchised whites that he was hanging with.

DIANA LEE INOSANTO It was beautiful seeing how my godfather created a community through martial arts. You had every colour under the sun with people from all different backgrounds. I loved how he talked about being a 'citizen of the Earth' and I think that's a really important concept to focus on, that we're all part of this global family. I feel lucky to have been able to get this kind of messaging at such a young age.

DOUG PALMER Bruce's classes were open to anyone who was interested in learning what he had to teach: male or female, young or old, of any ethnic background, with or without prior martial arts experience.

Bruce demonstrating at the Jun Fan Gung Fu
Institute, Seattle

DOUG PALMER I had spent the summer of 1963 in Hong Kong with Bruce and his family and we stopped off in Honolulu for a few days on our way back to Seattle.

During our stopover, Bruce was asked to give a demonstration to a gung fu school. He took me along to assist. There were 50 or so students and some instructors, all Chinese.

Afterwards one of the instructors came over to me. He was in his thirties or forties and had a cigarette dangling from his mouth. He asked if Bruce was teaching me. I realised that what he meant was, did Bruce teach to non-Chinese. I had been told by a Chinese classmate at Yale who was from Hawaii that only Chinese took gung fu there, and karate was mostly for Japanese. But not until the instructor asked me point blank after the demo did it sink in. Without thinking, I told him that Bruce taught anyone who was sincerely interested – 'even Chinese'.

Meanwhile a number of students had surrounded Bruce with additional questions, and the same instructor approached the group. He asked Bruce how he would block a straight kick. Bruce offered to demonstrate. The man delivered a straight kick to the groin, which Bruce blocked with a slap of his left hand to the top of the foot. Afterwards, Bruce spread his hands to indicate that that was the way to do the block. But the man hadn't withdrawn his foot all the way to the ground. He left it half-extended in the air, and as Bruce spread his hands the man gave his foot a little flick. 'See,' he said. 'You were open there.'

Bruce was smouldering, but didn't respond directly. He continued explaining various techniques and offered to demonstrate a different block. The man obliged and threw a punch, but this time Bruce did not withdraw after blocking it. He trapped the punch and threw a counter of his own, slow enough so that the man could easily block it with his free hand. As soon as he did, Bruce grabbed the hand and drew it down with a lap sau ('pulling hand'), effectively pinning both arms. The force and speed of the second pull was so great that the man's whole body jerked and the cigarette went flying out of his mouth. Bruce calmly continued his exposition for a while with the man's arms still pinned, demonstrating various follow-up punches with his free hand. Each time he demonstrated a follow-up manoeuvre the man's whole body would jerk again. Finally, his revenge complete, he let the man go.

Top: Bruce and friends in Honolulu, Hawaii,
16 August 1963
Above: Bruce and Doug Palmer, Hong Kong

SHANNON LEE He had a poster on the wall of his office, which is this fabulous design depicting two vultures sitting on a branch over a barren desert landscape with a cow skull on the ground, and it says, 'Patience, my ass! I'm gonna kill something!' So, of the yin and yang of Bruce Lee, that would be the yang side!

TED WONG I think that he had adapted a set of concepts and principles in his own martial art that many of us today are trying to follow.

MOZEZ Stillness is one of the fundamentals of Bruce Lee's teaching, to be in control of your emotion and to react only when necessary. This is true for life in general, not only from the perspective of fighting.

Top left: Poster from Bruce's office
Top right and above: Bruce in fighting stance at
home and in his office, 1966

DIANA LEE INOSANTO As children, Brandon and I would be running around the house of Uncle Bruce and Linda's and I would see this big library and there was my Uncle Bruce, my dad and all the students. There were a lot of important and poignant ideas being shared in those meetings. It was a community.

Left: Bruce at home reading *A Source Book in Chinese Philosophy*
Right: Books from Bruce's collection

BRUCE LEE If we examine the two clowns – the top dog and the underdog – that perform the self-torture game on the stage of our fantasy, then we usually find the two characters to be like this:

The Top Dog
The top dog usually is righteous and authoritarian; he knows best. He is sometimes right, but always righteous. The top dog is a bully and works with 'you should' and 'you should not'. The top dog manipulates with demands and threats of catastrophe, such as, 'If you don't … then you won't be loved, you won't get to heaven, you will die,' and so on.

The Underdog
The underdog manipulates with being defensive, apologetic, wheedling, playing the crybaby, and such. The underdog has no power. The underdog is Mickey Mouse. The top dog is the super-mouse. And the underdog works like this: 'I try my best. Look, I try again and again. I can't help it if I fail? I have such good intentions.' So you see the underdog is cunning, and he usually gets the better of the top dog because the underdog is not as primitive as the top dog.

So the top dog and underdog strive for control. Like every parent and child, they strive with each other for control. The person is fragmented into controller and controlled. This inner conflict, the struggle between the top dog and the underdog, is never complete, because the top dog as well as the underdog fights for his life.
   This is the basis for the famous self-torture game. We usually take for granted that the top dog is right, and in many cases the top dog makes impossible perfectionistic demands. So if you are cursed with perfectionism, then you're absolutely sunk. This ideal is a yardstick which always gives you the opportunity to browbeat yourself, to berate yourself and others. Since this ideal is an impossibility, you can never live up to it. You are merely in love with this ideal, and there is no end to the self-torture, to the self-nagging, self-castigating. It hides under the mask of 'self-improvement'. It never works.
   – Notes titled 'The Top Dog and the Underdog'

Bruce in Reserve Officers' Training Corps
uniform, Seattle, March 1961

BRUCE LEE How does one judge if an instructor is good? Rather, this question should be rephrased to read, how can one judge if a method or system is good? After all, one cannot learn the speed or power of an instructor, but one can access his skill. Thus the soundness of the system, and not the instructor, is to be considered. The instructor is merely there to point the way and lead his disciples to an awareness that he himself is the one and only one to give true feeling and expression to the system.

– *The Tao of Gung Fu, 1964*

DIANA LEE INOSANTO It's amazing how many people don't know the history of martial arts. They want to learn how to punch and kick and all the physical stuff, but they have no concept of the history and philosophy, which to me is a little scary. Today I see people out there doing martial arts and I can tell they lack a philosophy. That's never what my godfather was about.

W. KAMAU BELL As I read more of Bruce's writings, I realised that he's not just writing about the physicality, he's talking about how to live your life. I didn't end up being a high level martial artist but his quotes have stuck with me. The one that I quote the most is, 'Absorb what is useful, discard what is useless and add what is specifically your own.' As a comedian, a director and someone who cares about the world, that's my whole life. It is about creating my own path.

Top: Bruce and Taky Kimura, Seattle

Walking along the bank of Lake Washington

B. Lee 1963.

The breeze on the bank
Already blows cool and mild;
The distant merging of lake & sky
Is but a red trace of sunset.
The deep silence of the lake
Cuts off all tumult from me.
Along the lonely bank
I move with slow footstep:
Alone the disturbed frogs scurry off.
Here and there are houses,
Cool beads of light spring out from them.
A dazzling moon
Shines down from the lonely depths of
the sky.
In the moonlight slowly I move to
a Gung fu form.
Body and soul are fused into one.

BRUCE LEE
WALKING ALONG THE BANK OF LAKE WASHINGTON
1963

The breeze on the bank
Already flows cool and mild;
The distant merging of lake & sky
Is but a red trace of sunset.
The deep silence of the lake
Cuts off all tumult from me.
Along the lonely bank
I move with slow footsteps:
Alone the disturbed frogs scurry off.
Here and there are houses,
Cool beads of light spring out from them.
A dazzling moon
Shines down from the lonely depths of the sky.
In the moonlight slowly I move to a gung fu form.
Body and soul are fused into one.

BOATING IN LAKE WASHINGTON

I live in memory of a dream
Which has come and gone;
In solitude I sit on my boat
As it glides freely down the tranquil lake.
Across the blue sky, the swallows fly in couples;
On the still water, the mandarin ducks swim, side by side
Leaning on the oar I gaze at the water far away,
The sky far away, the loved one far away.

The sun goes down in flame on the far horizon; and
Soon the sunset is rushing to its height through
Every possible phase of violence and splendor.
The setting of the sun is supposedly a word of peace,
But a evening like the soft and invisible
Bonds of affection, adds distress to my heart.

Everything is now quiet and calm.
I look into the water; it is as clear as the night
When the clouds float past the moon,
I see them floating in the lake, and
I feel as though I were rowing in the sky.
Suddenly I think of you — mirrored so in my heart

Lying back on the boat,
I try to conjure up the land of dream where
I may seek for you.
But, alas, no dreams come, only
A moving point of fire in the dark,
The distant light of a passing boat.

BOATING

BRUCE LEE
BOATING ON LAKE WASHINGTON
1963

I live in memory of a dream
Which has come and gone;
In solitude I sit on my boat
As it glides freely down the tranquil lake.
Across the blue sky, the swallows fly in couples;
On the still water, the mandarin ducks swim, side
by side.
Leaning on the oar I gaze at the water far away,
The sky far away, the loved one far away.

The sun goes down in flame on the far horizon; and
Soon the sunset is rushing to its height through
Every possible phase of violence and splendor.
The setting of the sun is supposedly a word
of peace,
But an evening like the soft and invisible
Bonds of affection only adds distress to my heart.

Everything is now quiet and calm.
I look into the water; it is as clear as the night.
When the clouds float past the moon,
I see them floating in the lake, and
I feel as though I were rowing in the sky.
Suddenly I think of you – mirrored so in my heart.

Lying back on the boat,
I try to conjure up the land of dream where
I may seek for you.
But, alas, no dreams come, only
A moving point of fire in the dark,
The distant light of a passing boat.

Bruce on the dock of Lake Washington, Seattle

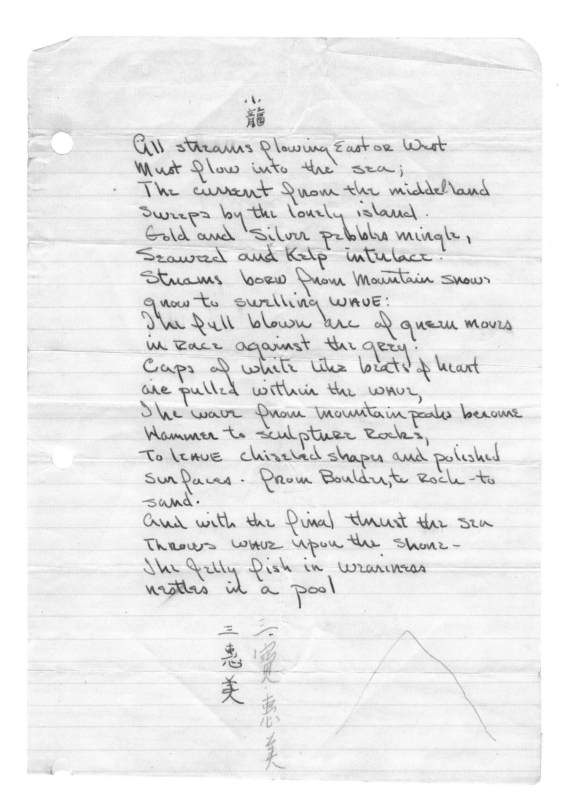

All streams flowing East or West
Must flow into the sea;
The current from the middelland
Sweeps by the lonely island.
Gold and Silver pebbles mingle,
Seaweed and Kelp interlace.
Streams born from Mountain snows
grow to swelling WAVE:
The full blown arc of green moves
in Race against the grey.
Caps of white like beats of heart
are pulled within the wave,
The wave from mountain peaks become
Hammer to sculpture Rocks,
To leave chiseled shapes and polished
Surfaces. from Boulder, to Rock — to
sand.
And with the final thrust the sea
Throws wave upon the Shore —
The frilly fish in weariness
nestles in a pool

SHANNON LEE I think my father's poetry aligned with the fact that he was a Chinese speaker. The Chinese language is very poetic and open to interpretation. For example, you will find Chinese people getting into quite a debate over the exact meaning of words and what it is they're trying to express. His poetry was about his own experiences and feelings. Expressing himself was a constant quest for him and, like his philosophical writings, he often wrote many drafts of the same poem.

BRUCE LEE When I enrolled in the University of Washington and was enlightened by philosophy, I regretted all my previous immature assumptions. My majoring in philosophy was closely related to the pugnacity of my childhood. I often ask myself these questions: What comes after victory? Why do people value victory so much? What is glory? What kind of victory is glorious?

– Newspaper article titled 'Me and Jeet Kune Do', 1972

The "Columns" at the University of Washington where Bruce asked Linda for the first date: October 25, 1963 to the Space Needle

SHANNON LEE My father was a very contemplative person. He had a keen intellect and a curious mind. Whether he had formally studied philosophy or not, he would have found his way there eventually.

Top left: University of Washington campus
Top right: Bruce at the University of Washington

SHANNON LEE The education my father received while at university was probably very Western, but interestingly he went to Garfield High School to guest lecture in Eastern philosophy. Being five years younger, my mom was actually a student there at the time, and it was where she first laid eyes on my father. She had a friend who told her that the same guy from Eastern philosophy also taught gung fu lessons. So they both signed up, and this was how my parents met. After gung fu classes they would all go out to lunch together, and one day my father asked my mom if she would like to go to the Space Needle, just the two of them. It was a very fancy venue back then and so it was a big deal to go. This was their first date.

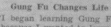

Bruce Lee, Chinese Movie Star, Speaks to Garfield Seniors

Gung Fu Is Way of Life as Well as Mode of Self-Defense, Lee Says

by CINDY THAL

Bruce Lee, 22 year old Chinese movie star, artist, Gung Fu master, and "Cha Cha King of Hong Kong", spoke recently at Garfield to a fascinated audience of seniors.

Although born in San Francisco, Bruce returned to China at the age of three months and received his education there. "Hong Kong is really nice," he said, "I plan to go back in March."

Mixture of Ancient China-Modern America

A psychology major at the University of Washington, Bruce thinks of himself as an Americanized Chinese.

Five feet, seven inches tall and 140 pounds, Bruce learned British English and the techniques of Gung Fu.

Gung Fu Changes Life

"I began learning Gung Fu at 13 because I wanted to learn how to fight. Now it has changed my whole life and I have a completely different way of thinking."

Taught by a Chinese master, the leader of the Wing-Chuing School of Gung Fu, Bruce, in five years became eligible as an instructor.

"I want to establish Gung Fu institutes throughout the United States and write books about it," said Bruce about his future plans.

Gung Fu is a way of life as well as a mode of self defense. It is based on Yin (negative) and Yang (positive) where everything is a complement. Examples are softness with firmness, night with day and man with woman. It is a quiet awareness of one's opponent's strength and plans, and how to complement them.

Linda in fighting demonstration with Taky Kimura and Bruce (annotation added by Bruce)

LINDA LEE CADWELL Bruce was constantly reading books that were geared towards positive thinking. He often motivated himself by referring to a certain book or a certain philosopher.

Bruce was always very positive because he was always moving forwards, he wasn't looking back.

BRUCE LEE Many philosophers are among those who say one thing and do another and the philosophy that a man professes is often quite other than the one he lives by. Philosophy is in danger of becoming more and more only something professed.

– *Essay titled 'Living: The Oneness of Things', circa 1963*

Top: Bruce and Linda, Seattle
Middle: Bruce and Linda at James Lee's house, Oakland, 1964
Bottom: Bruce outside Jun Fan Gung Fu Institute, Seattle, 1964

James,
glad to have received your letter and hear that you're training hard by yourself and Jimmy Ong.

This is the usual counter on that foot hook (Actually, by your measured distance, he shouldn't be able to come close in without being hit by 挿捶 or practically anything. ~~~

(一) (二) (三)

挿捶
(Horse Twisting)

elbow him (with left) while leading him back

right foot advances

In regarding to the 13 years old master from Formosa that is the reason for 黄淳梁 not opening the gym is a lot of bull. First of all, is this old master a nut? I mean does he go around and if he closing up 武館? If he does is really really good at his age, then

Mr. James Y. Lee
3039 Monticello Ave
Oakland 19,
California
U S A

Bruce Lee
218 Nathan Rd. 1/F
Kowloon, Hong Kong

LINDA LEE CADWELL I always say he's the most self-educated man that I've ever known in my lifetime, in many fields. Curiosity, creativity, imagination, finding different avenues – that was his nature.

SHANNON LEE Anything my father did, he tried to do to the best of his ability. His handwriting was beautiful, and that was very intentional. If he was going to write to someone, he was going to do it with artistry. For him, human connection was very important – he was a good friend. I think he found a lot of value in putting his thoughts to paper as well as trying to help people as much as possible. Friendships were an important touchpoint energetically for him.

DOUG PALMER Bruce's character and personal qualities were as important to his success as his physical attributes. He was self-disciplined and persistent to the point of being a perfectionist, dedicating hours of practice to master whatever he put his mind to, whether a martial arts technique or the cha-cha. He was self-confident, open-minded to new ideas and people, and willing to share. He had a flair for showmanship, a subtle sense of humour that could be self-deprecating, and a personal character that combined generosity, loyalty, a sense of dignity and a respect for others.

BRUCE LEE Every action should have its why and wherefore and there ought to be a complete and proficient theory to back up the whole concept of Chinese martial arts. I wish to infuse the spirit of philosophy into martial arts; therefore I insist on studying philosophy.

– *Newspaper article titled 'Me and Jeet Kune Do', 1972*

POWER TRAINING

Dear George,   June 25 1966

    It was nice of you to call.

    I'll probably come down one weekend in the middle of next month to pick up some of the weights. By the way, the grip machine you made for me is darn good, and it helps me in my training very much. If and when I make the trip, I will let you know, as I like to get together with you.

    Thanks again for your thoughtful call, and do drop me a line when you have the time.

    Take care my friend

Top: Bruce working out at home
Above: Typewritten letter to George Lee, thanking him for the grip machine he made which can be seen in bottom left corner of the photograph

EXERCISES & FORMS (special features)

❋ ~ method follows the "FLOW OF WATER" as running water never grows stale.

❋ ~ NON-STRENUOUS - serves to normalize instead to over-develop or to over-exert the body.

❋ ~ Movements ~~are graceful~~; can be practiced by both sexes, children or old people.

ABOVE ALL, GUNG FU DEVELOPS CONFIDENCE, HUMILITY, COORDINATION, ADADTABILITY, AND RESPECT TOWARDS OTHERS.

Things live by moving, and gain strength as they go

STEVE AOKI Talking about the human side of things, there are few cultural figures that have really changed the world by their words. Bob Marley is one of them, John Lennon is one of them and Bruce Lee is one of them. There are only a few people that can talk to people in a way that touches you to the soul. And you know how genuine and authentic and human it is. It's not about the martial art really; the martial art is an extension of his philosophy and the human side of everything. So when you get there, then you're a devout fan for life, you're changed forever.

BRUCE LEE Many people dedicate their lives to actualising a concept of what they should be like, rather than actualising themselves. This difference between self-actualising and self-image actualising is very important. Most people only live for their image.
– *Notes titled 'The Top Dog and the Underdog'*

DIANA LEE INOSANTO People always think of Uncle Bruce as an actor first. But he was a philosopher and martial artist first. If anything, his movies and his writings were all a reflection of his philosophy. They were his way of expressing himself as a human being.

Bruce working out at home in Barrington Plaza, Los Angeles, where he stayed during the filming of *The Green Hornet*

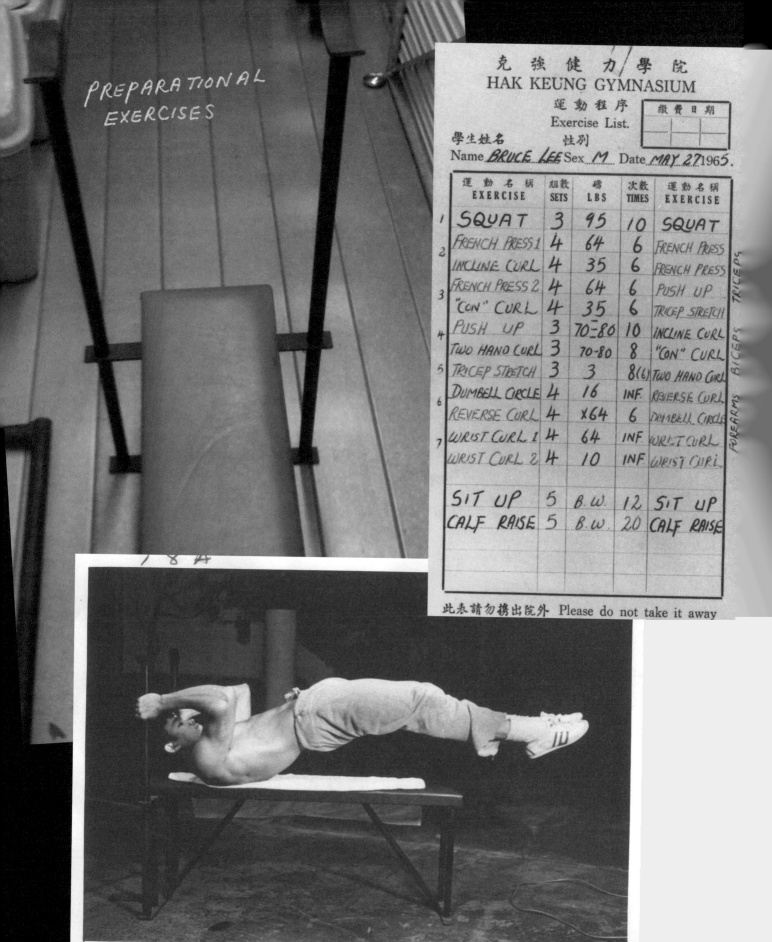

PREPARATIONAL EXERCISES

克 強 健 力 學 院
HAK KEUNG GYMNASIUM

運動程序
Exercise List.

繳費日期

學生姓名 性別
Name *BRUCE LEE* Sex *M* Date *MAY 27 1965.*

	運動名稱 EXERCISE	組數 SETS	磅 LBS	次數 TIMES	運動名稱 EXERCISE	
1	SQUAT	3	95	10	SQUAT	
2	FRENCH PRESS 1	4	64	6	FRENCH PRESS	
	INCLINE CURL	4	35	6	FRENCH PRESS	
3	FRENCH PRESS 2	4	64	6	PUSH UP	
	"CON" CURL	4	35	6	TRICEP STRETCH	
4	PUSH UP	3	70-80	10	INCLINE CURL	
	TWO HAND CURL	3	70-80	8	"CON" CURL	
5	TRICEP STRETCH	3	3	8(6)	TWO HAND CURL	
6	DUMBELL CIRCLE	4	16	INF.	REVERSE CURL	
	REVERSE CURL	4	X64	6	DUMBELL CIRCLE	
7	WRIST CURL 1	4	64	INF.	WRIST CURL	
	WRIST CURL 2	4	10	INF.	WRIST CURL	
	SIT UP	5	B.W.	12	SIT UP	
	CALF RAISE	5	B.W.	20	CALF RAISE	

FOREARMS BICEPS TRICEPS

此表請勿攜出院外 Please do not take it away

18 A

BRUCE LEE as Kato
VAN WILLIAMS as Britt Reid / Green Hornet
WENDE WAGNER as Lenore 'Casey' Case

BROADCAST 9 September 1966–17 March 1967

TV Star To Sign Autographs At IGA

Bruce Lee, familiar to television fans as Kato in "The Green Hornet", will sign autographs Saturday from 2 to 4 p.m. at the First Hill IGA Foodliner, 8th and Madison. Lee feels at home at this particular store, as one of the owners is Taky Kimura, an associate of his in establishing local Gung-Fu schools, for the instruction of simple self-defense.

It was while Kimura and Lee were gung-fu instructors that they decided to participate in the world karate tournament in Long Beach, California, in 1964. While at the tournament, Lee was "discovered" by TV scouts, and became involved in discussions that led to the "Green Hornet" series.

THE GREEN HORNET

THE GREEN HORNET

BEAUTIFUL DREAMER
TWO PARTER

WRITTEN BY

LORENZO SEMPLE, JR AND KEN PETTUS

EXECUTIVE PRODUCER

WILLIAM DOZIER

PRODUCER

RICHARD BLUEL

The Green Hornet, 1966–1967
Top left: Bruce reading the script for the
'Beautiful Dreamer' episode
Above: First US screen test for *The Green Hornet*
Opposite top: Fight scenes
Opposite middle: Letter from Fox Studios
detailing Bruce's role as Kato
Opposite bottom: Bruce and Van Williams on set

DIANA LEE INOSANTO Uncle Bruce weathered some amazing storms. My godfather was a product of World War II. He experienced a lot of racism as a child growing up in Hong Kong. He looked Asian but he was excluded at times because he was a quarter Caucasian of European descent. Then, as a young man going across to America, he had to deal with the opposite where he was excluded for being Asian.

It was a significant breakthrough for him to play the role of Kato in the TV show *The Green Hornet*. Back then in 1966, there were only three major television networks, and they were excluding people of colour from major roles. They primarily served Caucasian audiences and storylines.

Mr. Bruce Lee
2332 Eleventh East
Seattle, Washington 98102

Dear Bruce:

   Very many thanks for your note of November
sixteenth enclosing the suggestions from your friend,
Robert Pevonak. Some of them are very cogent and will
be useful as we go along in rounding out whatever
character we finally come up with for you.

   As Bill Belasco may have told you, my present
thinking is to feature you as Kato, the Oriental-ish
righthand man of the Green Hornet in the series of that
name which was on radio and in comic books for many years
and which we have just bought to put into production for
next season.

SPARRING

VAN WILLIAMS When we got in that Black Beauty and we got on our gear (thank God it wasn't a costume with a cape like Batman had to wear) we were partners. We were 50/50 partners.

BRUCE LEE To me a motion picture is motion. You've got to keep the dialogue down to a minimum.
– *The Pierre Berton Show, September 1971*

VAN WILLIAMS He was an honest kid that was very enthused about what he could do with his hands and feet. He was absolutely in love with martial arts and that's what he wanted to be a star of. He didn't care about being a star actor.

C-9813 – 1

C-9813 – 2

C-9813 – 4

Bruce and Van Williams

W. KAMAU BELL To me one of the greatest examples of white privilege in the history of mankind is the crossover episode 'Batman's Satisfaction'. At the time I thought it was stupid but now I realise it was white privilege. There's a scene at the end where the Green Hornet is squaring off against Batman and Kato is squaring off against Robin, and it was like really? This dude? Give him Batman, give him both of them! It's like handing Jimi Hendrix a broken ukulele.

It's very clear that Bruce is the guy with the charisma and the skills and yet he's standing there somewhat subservient to the other guys. This was the situation that black folks, Jewish folks and more found themselves in. We had to be ten times better than white people to get in the same place. And then we couldn't even show how good we were because we didn't want to make them look bad.

VAN WILLIAMS Burt Ward was absolutely petrified when he was going to work with [Bruce], and he didn't want to. Bruce got the script, and in the original script he lost to Robin. Well, that didn't go over too good with Bruce. He walked off the show. He said, 'I'm not going to do that.' He said, 'There's no way that anyone would believe I go in there and fight Robin and lose.'

Burt Ward (Robin), Adam West (Batman), Van Williams (the Green Hornet) and Bruce (Kato) filming the *Batman* episode 'Batman's Satisfaction', 1966

Opposite, top right: Bruce's notebook and sketch
This page and opposite: Bruce and Van Williams

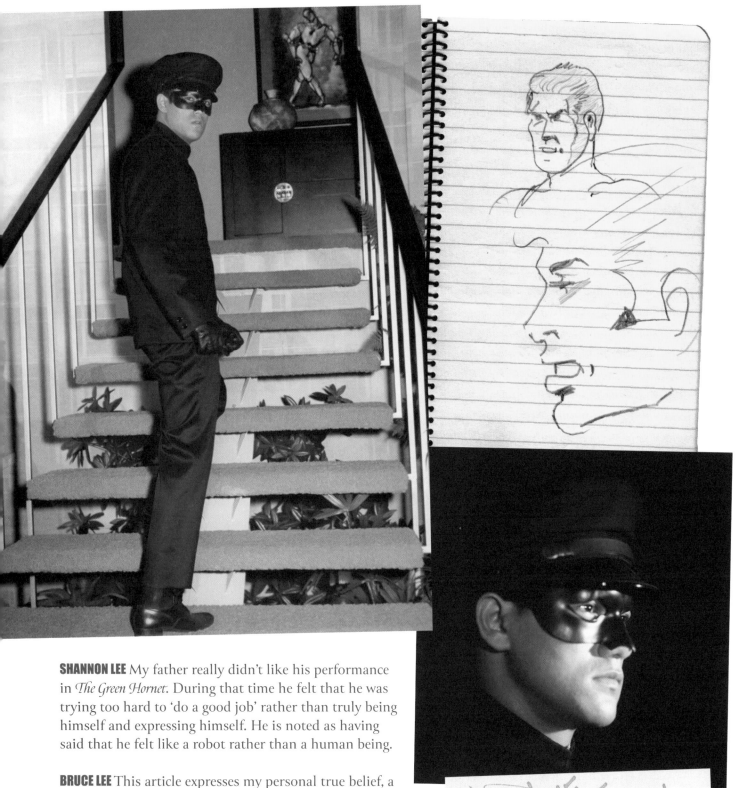

SHANNON LEE My father really didn't like his performance in *The Green Hornet*. During that time he felt that he was trying too hard to 'do a good job' rather than truly being himself and expressing himself. He is noted as having said that he felt like a robot rather than a human being.

BRUCE LEE This article expresses my personal true belief, a sort of personal view of the motion picture industry and the personal true belief of an actor as well as a human being. Above all, I have to take responsibility for myself and to do whatever is right. The script has to be right, the director has to be right, my time devoted towards preparation of the role. After that comes the money.

– Essay titled 'Another Actor Speaks His Mind', circa 1973

TAKY KIMURA When I first met [Bruce] I was 36 and he was 18. For some reason he picked me out to be his buddy. He was able to look into me and realise what was happening to me and he took it upon himself to help me along. He used to tell me, 'Hey, you're just as good as me.' I would always respond, 'Oh no, Sifu, I can't be as good as you!' But he helped me to ground myself and to recognise that we're all human beings – no more, no less than anybody else. Bruce was the guy that helped me regain my stature of who I am rather than being a Jap kid that was beat up and cussed out and everything else like that. The guy was such a charismatic person, he changed my whole life.

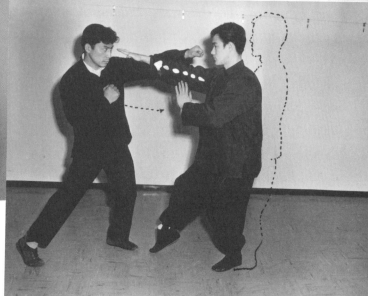

This page and opposite: Letter to Taky Kimura from Bruce about *The Green Hornet*
Above: Taky, Bruce and Charlie Woo, Seattle
Right: Bruce demonstrating with Taky (annotation added by Bruce)

sake, we better.

Next week I'm doing a pictorial layout of Gung Fu in color in the Dozer stadium for T.V. ~~guide~~ Guide.

You know, whether or not this show will go, the show will last at least till march. So Gung Fu will have enough exposure and so is Kato, Bruce Lee.

The schools will definitely go. I'll discuss with you in more detail. I'm preparing for it. Let's make use of this opportunity buddy.

Take Care   Bruce

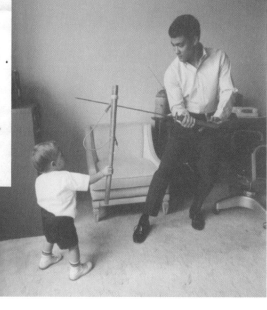

OPEN SEASON ON BRUCE LEE

BLAST HIM

Editor's Note: Since BLACK BELT published a two-part article on Bruce Lee (Green Hornet's "Kato") we have received a flood of letters concerning him and his style of Chinese Gung Fu. We reprint some of them here and, in cases applicable, Mr. Lee's replies to them.

Above: Bruce at home with Linda and Brandon

BRUCE LEE
IN MY OWN PROCESS
LETTER EIGHT (DRAFT)

Any attempt to write a 'meaningful' article – or else why write it at all – [about] how I, Bruce, emotionally feel or how I honestly react instinctively towards any matter is no easy task. I must stress here that this is purely my personal opinion but also my personal right. I do my own thing and you do yours. I am not here to please anybody. You are you and I am I, and if we communicate, fine and beautiful. If not, it cannot be helped anyway.

I must warn the reader that I am writing whatever wants to be written at the moment, so do not expect a nicely phrased and standardised and coherent type of intellectual article. Therefore, as I've just said, if we somehow communicate, I am most happy. After all, let's face it, as human beings we do have different levels of understanding and preferences. I accept it and expect it – that is if he is a genuine human being without his facade.

This article can certainly be made less demanding and definitely much easier should I indulge myself in the common manipulating game of role-playing or image-playing. To put it point blank – and that is me – I simply am not that type. What type? Well, I am the type constantly actualising my potentiality rather than portraying a mere image; which by the way is merely a ...

(Overleaf) AND what's more, I have to take responsibility for myself and accept the consequence of my own doing. I know, I am not being summoned to write a true confession, but I do want to be honest. Like I said, why write it at all if I'm trying to show off?

Ever since I was a kid I wanted quality – to be of quality I neither mean for the sake of the empty word quality nor 'quality for' but simply to be quality. Indeed we do not live forever. Quality demands total dedication, much sacrifice and in my case lots of painful constant practice of what one believes in.

I have come to accept life as a process, and am satisfied that in my ongoing process I am constantly discovering, expanding in martial art and especially in life, finding the cause of my ignorance. In short, to be real and to do my utmost to let other nationalities to appreciate us Chinese. After all, under the heaven there is but one family. I feel ready to fulfil my mission. How serious am I? [I would even] die for it.

Transcription of a draft (shown opposite) of
In My Own Process, the title Bruce gave to a series
of essays in which he reflected on his life

In my own process

Any attempt to write a "meaningful" article — or else why write it at all — here? Bruce, emotionally feel or consider honestly react instinctively toward any matter; its no on easy task. I must stress here that this is purely my personal opinion but also my personal right. I do my own thing and you do yours, I am not here to please anybody. You are you and I am I, if we communicate, fine and beautiful. If not, it cannot be helped anyway.

I must warn the readers that I am writing "whatever I want to be written at the moment. So do not expect a nicely phrased and standard and decent type of article. Therefore if we somehow communicate, I am most happy; after all, let's face it, as human beings, we do have different level of understanding and preferences. I accept it

This article can certainly less demanding and definitely must should I indulge myself in the common manipulating game of role or image playing. To put it point blank — and stick in me — I simply am not this type. What type? Well, I am the constantly actualizing myself rather than actualizing a mere image; which, by the way, is merely a

待人接物.
(一). 我們待人，並不是對待事講理性的動物，對方都是有情感，有偏見，有虛榮心和自尊之念的，所以我們不要妄自批評人們.
(二). 最好說話時先忘卻自己，事替人家著想，那就能夠確切地看出人家優点，然後不吝惜地說出來誇獎. 對方當然會覺得你的說話中他的心坎，而對你凜致好感，所以最好少說話，虛心下氣聽人說話
(三). 我們對人必須誠摯篤厚，誠意讚美人們長處，研究人家所愛好，迎合人的興趣，客氣，永遠露著笑容.
(四). 所使人歡喜的性質是
(1).愉快 (2)寬容 (3)真誠 (4)同情 (5)圓滑 (6)正直 (7)可信託 (8)謙恭 (9)自特 (10)樂於助人
(五). 他們歡喜感覺自己重要
" " " 向人示惠.
" " " 別人知道他們
" " " 他們被信任
" " " 他們特別癖好.
" " " 大家興趣一致
" " " 被人請教
" " " 向他們吐露心憶.
" " " 人家注意他們.

他們歡喜能賞識他們的人
(六). 要保持友情，不要無故爭吵，常常讚美他(她)們的衣服，常施小惠，有問題時不要口出怨言，不要指摘他(她)們的說話，關心他(她)們的一切，滿足他(她)們榮高心，不要妒嫉，盡情原諒.
(七). 好尊自大，是人所具有的心理，現像，我們必須抓住人家的這種心理善自利用，使他(她)們知道你對於他(她)們的優点，確是誠心感服，毫不虛飾.
(八). 頌揚他(她)幾声，排撥他(她)幾句. 介紹一個談話問題，在那時候你就可以發現他的興趣何在，他的意見書何？他的動作的主思處源，摯於何處？作進一步往他說話後面，含著怎樣的意絮.
(九). 常常說話，但不要說得太長，对什麼人說什麼話，少講故事，除非貼切而簡短，總以絕對太說為妙. 切不要拉住別人的衣袖或手來講話. 隨和對別人，不要妄獨斷自尊，在分子複雜的人象中，避免辯論，勿作自我宣傳，說話時正面視人，外表坦白而率直，內心謹慎而把細. 瞎児是最

SHANNON LEE My father wrote a lot about quality – doing a quality job and the importance of quality as a value to him. He equated quality to the concept of expressing your most cultivated and most 'real' self.

In letter four of *In My Own Process*, I love how he starts, 'What the hell? You are what you are and self-honesty occupies a definite and vital part in the ever-growing process to become a "real human being" and not a plastic one. Ever since I was a kid the word quality has meant a lot to me. Somehow I know I am devoting myself sincerely to it with much sacrifice and heading towards a direction, and you can rest assured that Mr Quality himself will always be there. Somehow, one day, you will hear, "Hey, now that's quality; here is someone real. I would like that."'

I just have to say, I think he did it!

Bruce's notes on social interaction, written in Chinese (translation opposite)

(1) When we interact with others, we are not dealing with animals that operate on pure logic. People have emotions, biases, vanities and feelings of self-esteem. Therefore, we should not presumptuously criticise them.

(2) When speaking to others, the best thing to do is to first forget yourself. Think only of the other person. That's how you can clearly see the other person's strengths. Then lavish them with effusive praise. Naturally, the other party will think what you're saying hits the nail on the head and will develop a good impression of you. That's why it's best to just talk less and humbly pay attention to others when they speak.

(3) We must treat other people with the utmost honesty and respect. Give sincere praise to the strength of others, study what they like, accommodate their interests, be polite, and always have a smile on your face.

(4) Personality traits that people like are:

(i) cheerfulness, (ii) forgivingness, (iii) honesty,

(iv) compassion, (v) worldliness, (vi) integrity,

(vii) trustworthiness, (viii) humility, (ix) self-control,

(x) helpfulness

(5) People all like:

> to feel that they are important
> to do favours for others
> to feel that others know of them
> to have their own little hobbies
> to think everyone has the same interests
> to be asked for advice by others
> when other people pour their hearts out to them
> other people to pay attention to them
> people who can appreciate them.

(6) In order to maintain a friendship with someone: don't pick fights for no reason; praise them often on their attire; do small favours for them; when there are problems don't just complain, don't point your fingers at what they're saying; satisfy their sense of being above it all; don't be envious; and forgive as much as possible.

(7) Pride and ego are psychological phenomena that are present in every person. We need to harness this kind of psychology and become good at using it. Let people know that you are truly impressed by their strengths, don't hide that at all.

(8) Praise them a bit, tease them a little. Start a topic of discussion. At that point you will be able to find where their interests lie, what their opinions are, the main source of their action, and where the hit is about to land. Then go even deeper and explore the real meanings that lie behind what they're saying.

(9) Speak often, but not for too long. Tailor what you're saying to who you're speaking to. Don't tell too many stories unless they are relevant and short. It's honestly best to not tell stories at all. Don't drag on people's sleeves or hands in order to talk to them. Be easygoing with other people, and don't be dogmatic and prideful. When you're among a complicated group of people, avoid debates. Do not promote yourself. When you're speaking look others in the eye. Present yourself on the surface as honest and straightforward, but inside you must be careful and pay attention to details. The worst and dumbest thing to do is to curse at someone. Laughing loudly is a rowdy form of entertainment.

(10) To have others agree with or relate to your opinions, you must listen to others, try not to be overanxious, and do not dominate the discussion. Always keep an open mind with honesty and listen to what others have to say. (Think more, talk less.)

  Note: A reliable way to pay detailed attention to other's emotions is to study their gestures and reactions and the way they conduct themselves.

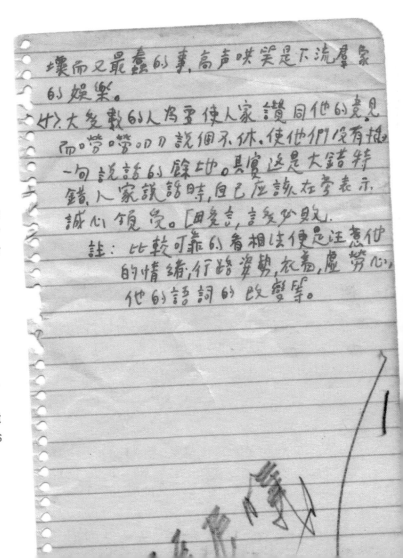

JEET KUNE DO 截拳道 **1967** 一九六七年

BRUCE LEE'S

ULTIMATE REALITY

OF

GUNG FU

JUN FAN GUNG FU INSTITUTE

振藩國術館

會員證

MEMBERSHIP CARD.

"USING NO WAY AS WAY; HAVING NO LIMITATION AS LIMITATION"

BRUCE LEE
IN MY OWN PROCESS
LETTER EIGHT

By martial art, I mean, like any art, it is an
unrestricted athletic expression of an individual
soul. Oh yes, martial art also means daily hermit-
like physical training to upgrade or maintain one's
quality. However, martial art is also about the
unfolding of the bare human soul. That is what
interests me.

FROM A RIGHT STANCE
KICKS

A) Side Kick

1) Downward side kick — shin to *side to*
   — shin/knee/high
   (1) R simple, knee/shin
   (2) R simple side to thigh/rib
2) parallel side kick — ribs, stomach *to rib*
   — kidneys
   (3) R simple side to head
   (4) Angle in high side(to L Stance)
   (5) Angle in low side (to L Stance)
3) upward side kick — head, solar *REVERSE*
   — plexus, head
   6) Forward L side
   8) LEAPING SIDE KICK
   9) JUMPING SIDE KICK
   9)a dropping side kick
   10) sliding side kick *LANDING*

B) Straight Kick

1) R high *straight*
2) R medium *straight*
3) R low *straight*
4) R angle in(to L Stance)
5) JKD groin kick
6) Double kicking
7) R. upward kick (a).- knee
               (b).- wrist
10). step back straight

C) Hook Kick

1) R simple high hook
2) "   "   medium hook
3) "   "   low hook
4) L simple high hook *reverse*
5) L simple medium hook
6) L " " low
7) R one-two hook
8) L "-" "
9). jumping hook.
10) step back hook
11). Double leaping hook THREE FOOT SWEEPS

D) Spin KICK *R back*

1) L simple spin, high *back*
2) L "   "   low *hook*
3) L "   "   medium JUMPING REVERSE SPIN
4) Advance two steps R spin
5). Step back spin

E) SIMPLE HEEL KICK
[STIFF LEGGED OR BENT]

1) R simple high heel
2) "   "   medium "
3) "   "   low   "
4) R one-two heel
5) L one-two heel (to left stance)
   reverse

F) FORWARD STRAIGHT KICK *REVERSE*

   reverse L straight
1) R simple high forward thrust
2) R "   medium " "
3) L "   low   " "
4) L reverse angle in high
5) L "   angle in medium
6) L "   low
7). Reverse L cross stomp
10). step back reverse straight

BRUCE LEE I do not believe in styles. I do not believe that there is such a thing as a Chinese way of fighting or a Japanese way of fighting because unless human beings have three arms and four legs, we will have a different form of fighting of course. But we have two hands and two feet. Styles separate men because they have their own doctrines and then the doctrine becomes the gospel truth that you cannot change. But if you don't have a style, you can say, here I am as a human being – how can I express myself, totally and completely? That way you won't create a style. Style is a crystallisation, and by removing that you can have a process of continuing growth.
– *The Pierre Berton Show, September 1971*

TAKY KIMURA I think Bruce Lee had a message when he taught. One of the goals that he was trying to achieve was the equality of people from different ethnic backgrounds but, on the other hand, Bruce was trying to show us a way in which we could make ourselves better people.

Top left and opposite: notes on Jeet Kune Do
Top right: Promotional photograph
Above: Photoshoot outtake

JEET KUNE DO 截拳道

PRIMARY FREEDOM :- a "frame" can kill the life of the situation by too rigid limitation

Forms & prearranged sparring are means to shield oneself from facing reality in its suchness

The "ISENESS" (FLUIDITY) is the primary freedom

Dissolve like a thawing ice (It has form) into water (formless and capable to fit in with anything)

When you have no form, you can be all form, when you have no style, you can fit in with any style 空

In Primary Freedom one utilizes all ways and is bound by none, and likewise uses any technique or mean which serves its end.

Enter a mould without being caged in it, obey the laws and principle without being bound by them.

To be at an "undifferentiated center" of a circle that has no circumference

Primary Freedom is the hinge of the pendulum which swings between the pro and con

Not neutrality, not indifference but transcendence is the thing needed.

The wheel revolves when it is not too tightly attached to the axle.

With all the training thrown to the wind, with a mind perfectly unaware of its own workings, with the self vanishing nowhere. anybody knows, the art of Jeet Kune Do attains its perfection

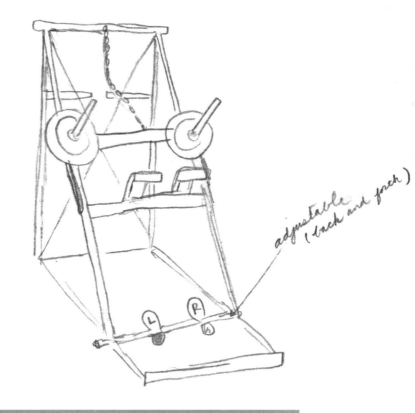

Above and top left: Bruce working out at home
Top right: Hand-drawn design for a weight machine (much of Bruce's workout equipment was made by his friend George Lee)

adjustable
(back and forth)

KAREEM ABDUL-JABBAR After my sophomore year at UCLA, I started studying martial arts and I started in aikido. I studied aikido that summer and when I came back to LA I wanted to continue my martial arts studies on the side, so I went over to *Black Belt* magazine and Mitoshi Uyehara, who was a friend of Bruce, was the editor. I said, 'Where's a good aikido dojo I can go to? I want to continue, not get rusty.' He told me that he could get me all the listings but there is a guy doing his own thing and that I might have seen him on TV as Kato. I knew a little bit about him but I hadn't seen *The Green Hornet* but I said that I'd like to meet him.

Bruce was living in Culver City and I went over to his house. It blew me away. He was so down to earth. So many martial arts instructors had this air about them that they were so important and they were into this other state of mind, but he was very approachable. He was a lot of fun. The difference between him and the other guys teaching martial arts was like night and day. He knew the practical things to teach you, he wasn't tied down by any traditional nonsense. He told me that anything I did had to work, otherwise it was useless. He was just so very clear and unpretentious, which I loved. He was the real thing. I trained with him and he liked the fact that I was in shape. I used to run with him after he moved up near Mulholland Drive.

Bruce, Dan Inosanto and students, including Kareem Abdul-Jabbar, at the Jun Fan Gung Fu Institute, Los Angeles, 1968

STEVE AOKI As I got older, I wanted to learn more than just his fighting techniques. I would get together with my friends who were also obsessed with Bruce Lee and we would watch the interviews and read the *Tao of Jeet Kune Do* and buy the books and read the philosophy. That was the next layer that put you deeper into the psyche of this man. It's one thing to like someone because of his fighting skills but it's another to see that there's a philosophy behind it that you can apply to your everyday life. And it's poetic and beautiful. Every time he spoke I would shudder because it was like poetry. He was like the first Asian rapper without a beat!

Bruce with Linda and Brandon, experimenting
with a Super 8 film camera

Did I invent a new style?

I ~~do not~~ deny that JKD is a style or a school, and that it is confined to the Chinese. In fact, to define JKD in term of a particular geographical structure or system is to miss it entirely. What cannot be "constructed" _ _ _ _ _ _ _ _ _ _

JKD cannot be set within distinct limit or ~~scheme~~ can be recognized as apart from this style or that style.

JKD is neither oppose to styles nor not-opposed to them.

JKD :- employ minimum of form (without being attached to it And is therefore free from it)

— the theme is for us to throw away all binding and be aware.

If you blindly follow a pattern, pretty soon you might understand some dead routine, but you do not understand yourself.

SECOND-hand artist

Pretty soon one is doing his methodical routine as response rather than simply responding.

A JKD man "listens" to Circumstance

A classical man "recite" his Circumstance,

Bruce's notes on Jeet Kune Do

DIANA LEE INOSANTO As a little girl I grew up calling him Uncle Bruce because he was a godfather figure in my life. My father, Dan Inosanto, included the 'Lee' in my name to honour him since he was a dear friend, teacher and Sifu (master). My father was a key instructor under my godfather at the Chinatown school in Los Angeles. He had to vet potential students because if Uncle Bruce ever overheard that a student wanted to use martial arts just to be vengeful or to 'kick ass', those students would not be accepted. It's important to understand that the hand of friendship is always going to be higher than the hand of war.

If you're a good instructor you should be able to teach your students when to walk away from a fight, where to use your intellect instead of acting in anger with one's fists. It's about being able to communicate and express yourself first to deescalate a situation. Of course, there are times when a person may have no choice but to defend oneself, but this was the philosophy I was given growing up.

W. KAMAU BELL I did martial arts for a long time because of Bruce Lee. You learn how to fight so that hopefully you'll fight less. You'll see the fight coming from across the street and you'll avoid it. You're not going to stand there and wait for the fight. Beating people up shouldn't be something you take pleasure in if you're a true martial artist. I think a lot of people get into martial arts for the wrong reasons – it's good to protect yourself but it's not good to beat people up.

Left: Bruce, Dan Inosanto and students at the
Jun Fan Gung Fu Institute, Los Angeles
Right and opposite: Jeet Kune Do photoshoot
featuring Bruce and Dan Inosanto

SHANNON LEE My father's art of Jeet Kune Do is very much the style of no style, the form of no form. The tenets of it are simplicity, directness and freedom. He was really into this notion that styles separate and limit people. They limit thinking, creativity and growth. Through exchange and direct engagement, he would learn about somebody else but also learn about himself; he never wanted to limit himself or what he could learn. He saw martial arts as a self-knowledge tool. He said everything he learned about life, he learned through the practice of martial arts. And he thrived on the process of knowing himself and then expressing that out in the world.

JEET KUNE DO

------toward personal liberation.

BRUCE LEE To me, ultimately martial arts means expressing yourself. That is very difficult to do. It is easy for me to put on a show and be flooded with a cocky feeling and feel pretty cool. Or I can do all sorts of phony things and do fancy movements, but to express oneself honestly, not lying to oneself, is very hard to do. You have to train, you have to get your reflexes so when you want it it's there. When you want to move you are moving, and when you move you are determined to move. If I want to punch, I'm going to do it. That is the sort of thing you have to train yourself to think and do.

– *The Pierre Berton Show, September 1971*

Top: Bruce demonstrating an eye jab with one of his students, Dan Lee, 1966
Above: Workout with Ted Wong at Linda Palmer's home, 1971

Bruce Lee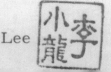

SIMPLICITY IS THE KEY

Fitness Program :—

(1) # Basic Fitness Exercises :—
    1). Alternate Split
    2). Run In Place.
    3). ~~Push ups~~ Jumping Squat
Everyday opportunities: push up
                                                    put shoes.
    1). Stairs   2). standing (one legged) (snap)
    3). ~~Stand~~ Walk 4). Quiet Awareness.

(2) Waist :—   1) waist twist @ 3 ½   (t) stick
               2). Side bend.
               3). forward & backward.
(3) STOMACH :— 1). Side sit-up.
               2). leg raise.
(4) SHOULDER :— 1). Roll.
               2). circling & swing.
(5) LEG —   1). t ½.
               2). knee turning
               3). high kick.

1). Alternate Splits. — (agility, leg. endurance)
2). waist twisting   (external obliques)
3). Run in place   (agility, endurance, leg.)
4). shoulder circling. (flexibility)
5). high kicks raise (flexibility)
6). ~~shoulder rotation~~   (") —— waist twisting
      side kick raise
                leg stretch (straight/side)
7). ~~sit up~~ ~~side kick raise~~ (")
8). sit up.   (rectus abdominus upper)
9). leg raises (" " lower)

The Art of Jeet Kune DO is simply to simplify.

Above left: Bruce weight-training
Above right: Bruce's fitness programme

Taky. Your concluding statement in your last letter was well spoken — "Your faith in me is my faith in" — rest assure that I do have faith in you, or else nothing as high as a fifth rank be granted to you.

You're right in the latest issue in Black Belt. I did help them — to raise the sad level of the Chinese arts a little. Did you also read the editorial?

Joe Lewis swallowed his pride and called for instruction — like Norris, Stone, I'll take him for a few lessons to establish the fact that he did come to me. All three of them are under me now.

Keep your newly promotion proudly, and let it be the reason for more training and further application.

I hope to see you somewhere in March. At that time. I'll get together with you for the the most important — Jeet Kune Do session in your entire training.

Take Care.

Bruce

JOE LEWIS Bruce came running out to me one day and said he wanted to talk to me. For about half an hour he was explaining that his Jeet Kune Do meant 'way of the stopping fist'. He was talking about throwing vertical punches instead of horizontal; instead of putting your power side back like a boxer, you should put your power side forward. He told me about many of the principles and tactics that Jeet Kune Do demonstrated or utilised which made it superior to the way we were doing karate at that time. It just went in one ear and out the other. But later in 1968 I was doing a nightclub act with Bob Wall, a co-star on *Enter the Dragon*, and Mike Stone. We were buddies at the time. At the end of each night Mike and I would do a demonstration of a karate match and I noticed his style had changed. He told me that he had been working with this Chinese guy named Bruce Lee and that Bruce also wanted to work with me and so he recommended that I go and take lessons with him. So eventually took Mike's advice and once a week I would go and practise with Bruce and spend

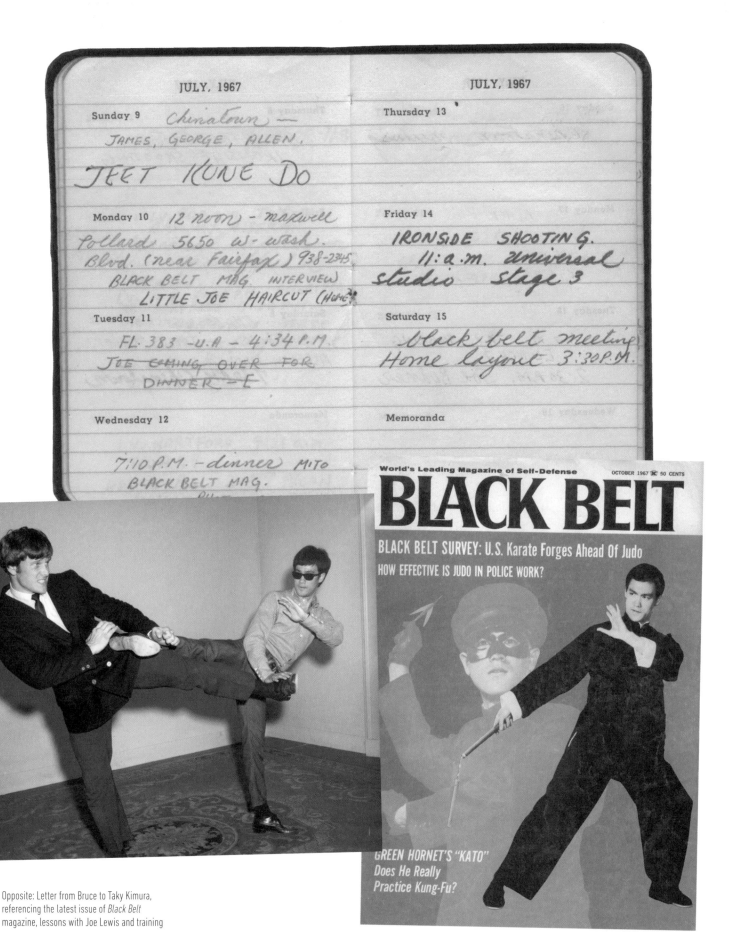

JULY, 1967

Sunday 9 — Chinatown —
JAMES, GEORGE, ALLEN,
JEET KUNE DO

Monday 10 — 12 noon — Maxwell
Pollard 5650 W. Wash.
Blvd. (near Fairfax) 938-2345
BLACK BELT MAG. INTERVIEW
LITTLE JOE HAIRCUT (Home)

Tuesday 11
FL. 383 — U.A — 4:34 P.M.
JOE COMING OVER FOR
DINNER — E

Wednesday 12
7:10 P.M. — dinner MITO
BLACK BELT MAG.

JULY, 1967

Thursday 13

Friday 14
IRONSIDE SHOOTING.
11: a.m. universal
studio stage 3

Saturday 15
Black belt meeting
Home layout 3:30 P.M.

Memoranda

World's Leading Magazine of Self-Defense   OCTOBER 1967 **K** 50 CENTS

BLACK BELT

BLACK BELT SURVEY: U.S. Karate Forges Ahead Of Judo
HOW EFFECTIVE IS JUDO IN POLICE WORK?

GREEN HORNET'S "KATO"
Does He Really
Practice Kung-Fu?

Opposite: Letter from Bruce to Taky Kimura,
referencing the latest issue of *Black Belt*
magazine, lessons with Joe Lewis and training

Top: 1967 day planner detailing meetings with
Black Belt magazine (featured right)
Above: Publicity photo with Joe Lewis

BRUCE LEE Let it be understood once and for all that I have not invented a new style, composite or modification. I have in no way set Jeet Kune Do within a distinct form governed by laws that distinguish it from 'this' style or 'that' method. On the contrary, I hope to free my comrades from bondage to styles, patterns and doctrines.

What, then, is Jeet Kune Do? Literally, 'jeet' means to intercept or to stop; 'kune' is the fist; and 'do' is the way, the ultimate reality – the way of the intercepting fist. Do remember, however, that 'Jeet Kune Do' is merely a convenient name. I am not interested with the term itself; I am interested in its effect of liberation when JKD is used as a mirror for self-examination.

– Essay titled 'Jeet Kune Do: What It Is Not', circa 1971

© 1967 by Bruce Lee
JEET KUNE DO 武 拳 道
(The 'Way' of The 'Stopping Fist')
CHINESE BOXING
from the
JUN FAN GUNG FU INSTITUTE

Basic Defense

1. Stop Hit --- Jeet Da

    A. Back stop kick .... Hou Jeet Tek
    B. Straight Stop Kick........ Jik Jeet Tek
    C. Hook Stop Kick .... O'ou Jeet Tek
    D. Side Stop Kick .... Juk Jeet Tek
    E. Vertical Fist............. Ch'ung Chuie
    F. Finger Jab .... Biu Jee

NOTE: In Jun Fan Gung Fu, there is no passive blocking. Instead of blocking a punch we usually use a stop hit to any place on the human body. A stop hit can be any kick or any punch.

2. Foot Obstruction, Stop Kick .... Jeet Tek

3. 4 Corners (Stop Hit with Parry)

    A. Right stop hit with high inside cover   Tan Da.

    B. Right stop hit with cross hand cover   Woang Pak Da

    C. Right stop hit with low inside cover   Loy Ha Pak Da

    D. Right stop hit with low outside cover   Ouy Ha Pak Da

See Foo .... Instructor
Sea Hing .... Your senior, your older brother
Sea Dai .... Your junior, your younger brother.
Sea Jo .... Founder of the style and system
Sea Bak .... Instructor's senior
See Sook .... Instructor's Junior
Sea Gung .... Grandfather, your instructor's instructor

Top left: Bruce and his brother Robert
Top right: Bruce and Dan Inosanto
Above: Notes on Jeet Kune Do

them we will become bound by their limitation. Remember, <u>you</u> are 'expressing' the technique and not 'doing' the technique. When someone attacks you it is not technique number one (or is it technique number two, stance two, section four?) that you are doing, but the moment you 'aware' his attack you simply move in like sound and echo without any deliberation. It is as though when I call you you answer me or when I throw something to you you catch it, that's all.

© 1967
by Bruce Lee

LINDA LEE CADWELL Whether Eastern or Western, ancient or modern, boxing or fencing, he studied all kinds of martial arts. And he drew from different areas those things that were useful to him, and rejected what was not, and adapted certain techniques to his own way of doing something. His Jeet Kune Do was all about the way *he* did it.

Above left: At-home workout
Above right: Bruce, Linda and Brandon at the Jun Fan Gung Fu Institute in Chinatown, Los Angeles

Explanation for the three signs (same black shining background as the sign you made)

FIRST SIGN

here all we need is one red half and one gold half of the Yin Yang symbol. HOWEVER __no__ dot is need on either halves; in other word it is just plain red with no gold dot, or just plain gold with no red dot (this serves to illustrate extreme softness (like 太極) or/and extreme hardness (like 洪家). So just follow the drawing and also put the phrase — PARTIALITY — THE RUNNING TO EXTREME on the black board

SECOND SIGN

Exact yin yang symbol like the sign you made for me except there is __no__ chinese characters around the symbol. Of course, the phrase — FLUIDITY — THE TWO HALVES OF ONE WHOLE will be on the black board.

THIRD SIGN

Just a shinny black board with nothing on it except the phrase EMPTINESS — THE FORMLESS FORM.

The three signs have to be the same size because they illustrate the three stages of cultivation. Please do make them like the sign you made for me aluminum and symbol and shinny black board

Bruce's notes explaining the three symbols representing Jeet Kune Do (pictured opposite)

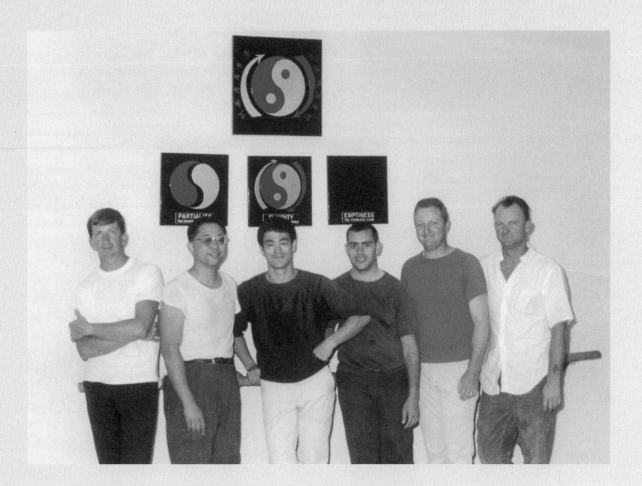

BRUCE LEE Firmness (yang) and gentleness (yin) are two complementary and interdependent facets of gung fu. It is because one singles out firmness and looks at it as distinct from softness that the idea of opposite is formed. Once a distinction is made about something, that certain something will suggest its opposite.

Harmony was regarded as the basic principle of the world order; as a cosmic field of force, in which the yin and the yang are eternally complementary and eternally changing. European dualism sees physical and metaphysical as two separate entities, at best as cause and effect, but never paired like sound and echo, or light and shadow, as in the Chinese symbol of all happening: the yin and the yang.

The dualistic philosophy reigned supreme in Europe, dominating the development of Western science. But with the advent of atomic physics, findings based on demonstrable experiments were seen to negate the dualistic theory and the trend of thought since then has been back towards the monistic conception of the ancient Taoists.

– Essays titled 'The Union of Firmness and Softness' and 'Taoism'

SHANNON LEE The symbol that represents Jeet Kune Do and Bruce Lee's approach to life is a full yin yang symbol surrounded by arrows. The arrows represent the constant interplay of the complements of yin and yang. The Chinese phrase surrounding the symbol translates to: using no way as way; having no limitation as limitation.

Bruce with students at the Jun Fan Gung Fu Institute, Los Angeles, 1967 (left to right: Jerry Poteet, Dan Lee, Bruce, unknown student, Pete Jacobs and Bob Bremer)

TED WONG I think Bruce Lee was more or less a self-taught martial artist. He dared to challenge the old system and he thought that the traditional and classical way of training martial artists was not the way to go. By doing so he more or less modernised martial arts today by using a modern scientific approach and constant research to develop a fighting system that he called Jeet Kune Do.

I learned a lot from him, just from how to generate speed alone. If any instructor could teach speed I think it was Bruce.

Top left: Bruce in Jeet Kune Do pose
Top right: Ted Wong's certificate from Bruce's
Jun Fan Gung Fu Institute
Above: Bruce demonstrating with Ted Wong

Top: Jeet Kune Do sketches and Chinese notations
Above: Bruce working out at home

BRUCE LEE Martial arts has a very deep meaning as far as my life is concerned: as an actor, as a martial artist, as a human being – all these I have learned from martial arts. Martial arts includes all the combative arts like karate, kung fu, judo, Chinese gung fu, boxing, aikido. It's the combative form of fighting.

All type of knowledge, ultimately, means self-knowledge. So, therefore, what I teach is not so much how to defend yourself or how to hurt somebody. Rather, when people want me to teach them they want to learn how to express themselves through movement, be it anger, be it determination or whatever. So they pay me to show them in combative form the art of expressing the human body.

– *The Pierre Berton Show, September 1971*

BRANDON LEE He trained me as soon as I could walk. After he passed away I kept at it. I didn't really think about it much. My dad had a circle of students that were close to him and were friends of the family and one of those men, Danny Inosanto, continued to be my teacher so that was kind of a nice unbroken line. I hadn't done it with any thought of getting into martial arts movies, but I had the skill and I happened to get into films that gave me the opportunity to use it.

Bruce and Brandon

DAN INOSANTO Bruce told me that you want to research, you want to experiment, then you want to develop something for you, and finally you have to develop something that will work for the majority of your students, because what works for one individual may not work for another individual.

DIANA LEE INOSANTO What I loved about my godfather and father is that they were researchers, a bit like mad scientists. They were passionate about self-discovery through the martial arts. They wanted to understand what the other arts could unlock for them.

There was a feeling among a lot of Asian groups coming over to America that it was important to keep the arts within their community and not to teach outsiders. However, my godfather felt it was important for cultures to share and bridge new understandings, bringing people together. My godfather and father examined French savate, fencing, kendo, Russian sambo, Indian martial arts, African martial arts and more because they wanted to explore. In learning these arts, you also learn about other people's heritage.

Photoshoot on the beach with Dan Inosanto
Drawing by Bruce

BRUCE LEE I am the first to admit that any attempt to crystalise Jeet Kune Do into a written article is no easy task. Perhaps to avoid making a 'thing' out of a 'process'. I have not until now personally written an article on JKD. Indeed, it is difficult to explain what Jeet Kune Do is, although it may be easier to explain what it is not.

Let me begin with a Zen story. The story might be familiar to some, but I repeat it for its appropriateness. Look upon this story as a means of limbering up one's senses, one's attitude and one's mind to make them pliable and receptive.

A learned man once went to a Zen teacher to inquire about Zen. As the Zen teacher explained, the learned man would frequently interrupt him with remarks like, 'Oh, yes, we have that too ...' and so on. Finally the Zen teacher stopped talking and began to serve tea to the learned man. He poured the cup full, and then kept pouring until the cup overflowed. 'Enough!' the learned man once more interrupted. 'No more can go into the cup!' 'Indeed, I see,' answered the Zen teacher. 'If you do not first empty the cup, how can you taste my cup of tea?'

– Essay titled 'Towards Personal Liberation (Jeet Kune Do)', circa 1971

Bruce demonstrating his famous two-finger
pushup, Dominican Republic, 1970

DIANA LEE INOSANTO 'Empty your cup' is a philosophy that stands out to me. It's about being open-minded, and it is important to me because when I philosophically empty my cup, I find that, all of a sudden, I get to be this sponge that can absorb new information and knowledge. I've applied this principle in learning to act and direct films. I've applied it in martial arts too. Even when meeting people that might be different in their viewpoints, I try to 'empty my cup' and listen.

BRUCE LEE In Jeet Kune Do one does not accumulate but eliminates. It is not daily increase, but daily decrease. The height of cultivation always runs to simplicity. It is the half-way cultivation that runs to ornamentation. So it is not how much fixed knowledge one has accumulated; rather it is what one can apply 'alively' that counts. 'Being' is definitely more valued than 'doing'.

– Student handout notes, circa 1967

Left: Illustrations of fighting techniques
Right: Bruce demonstrating with nunchucks

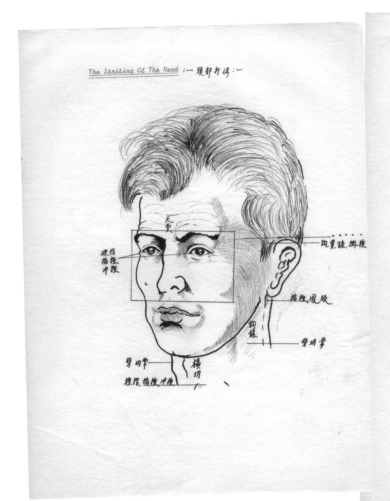

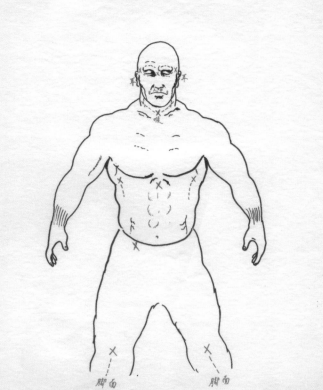

KAREEM ABDUL-JABBAR He was so competitive but he did it in the right way. He didn't try to put other people down. He was always about lifting himself and showing other people how to lift themselves. He just was able to take it so far. It really helped me with my basketball career, just to understand every day you have to be at your best.

BRUCE LEE Size is never a true indication of muscular power and efficiency. The smaller man usually makes up for the imbalance of power by his greater agility, flexibility, speed of foot and nervous action.

– *Essay titled 'Psychology in Defense and Attack', circa 1961*

Above: Illustrations identifying striking points on the head and body
Right: Bruce demonstrating isometric training at his home, Los Angeles

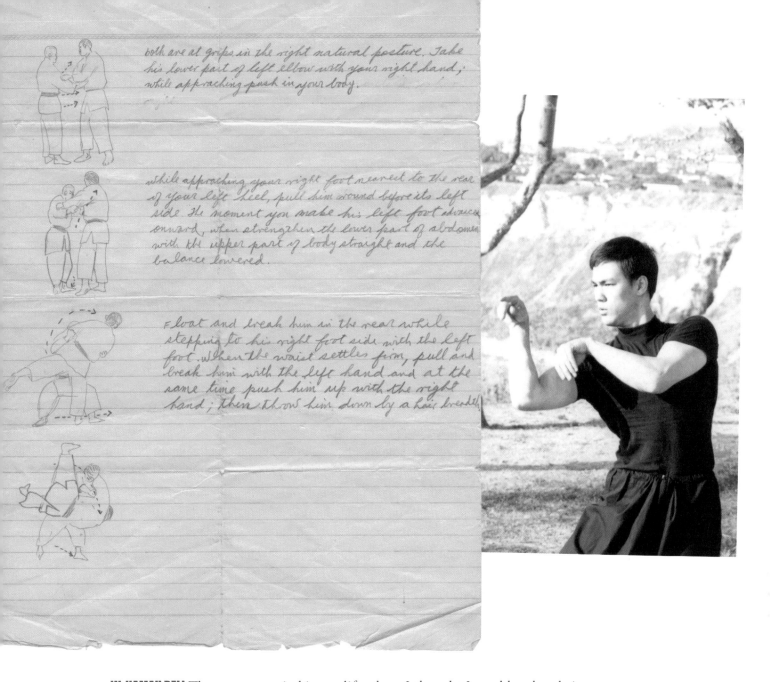

both are at grips in the right natural posture. Take his lower part of left elbow with your right hand; while approaching push in your body.

while approaching your right foot nearest to the rear of your left heel, pull him around before its left side. The moment you make his left foot advance onward, when strengthen the lower part of abdomen with the upper part of body straight and the balance lowered.

Float and break him in the rear while stepping to his right foot side with the left foot. When the waist settles firm, pull and break him with the left hand and at the same time push him up with the right hand; then throw him down by a hair breadth.

W. KAMAU BELL There was a period in my life where I thought I would end up being a professional martial artist, and when I didn't do that there was a part of me that felt like I'd almost let Bruce Lee down. But it became clear to me that it's about finding your own path and really going for it to achieve the best version of yourself. For Bruce Lee, martial arts was his medium. A lot of the time your heroes can inspire you either to do what they're doing or be a better version of yourself.

JEFF CHANG Martial arts has this dialectic between creativity and violence – it's literally in the name: war and art. These are war arts, arts that train people to defend themselves, yes, but the idea is also to be aggressive. Bruce's style, the intercepting fist, is not about going out and imposing yourself on other people. Built into this idea of Jeet Kune Do is the idea of intercepting an attack. It's self-defence. But, as we know, one person's self-defence is somebody else's aggression. So there is this fundamental contradiction when we're talking about martial arts.

Left and opposite top: Illustrations and notes on fighting forms
Right: Bruce in fighting pose

guarding right swing to face and
upper-cutting left to chin

leaning away from punch at face
and getting into position to send either
hand to body or face

Blocking left at body with right
elbow and launching left upper-
cut at jaw

side-step left against a left
lead to head

Ducking under a left swing
and sending left to solar plexus

Dodge and right hand cross counter against
straight left lead to face

BRUCE LEE There is no standard in total combat, and expression must be free. This liberating truth is a reality only in so far as it is 'experienced and lived' by the individual himself; it is a truth that transcends styles or disciplines. Remember, too, that Jeet Kune Do is merely a term, a label to be used as a boat to get one across; once across, it is to be discarded and not carried on one's back.

– *Essay titled 'Jeet Kune Do: What It Is Not', circa 1971*

TAKY KIMURA When Bruce was in the class teaching he had complete attention from all of us. He worked us until we dropped almost. We just thoroughly enjoyed and respected it. It was like reading the Bible – we swore by it. He was a person that when he told you he was going to teach you something, if you had any doubt in your mind whether it was going to work or not, he personally showed you why it would work and there was not an ounce of doubt that what he taught you was completely useful.

Above: Fighting positions and notes
Right: Anatomical notes

DOUG PALMER He was also open to learning new techniques from those with a different martial arts background and was able to quickly incorporate them into his arsenal. That's why he attracted students that were decades older than he was and had already experienced the martial arts, like James Lee and others.

BRUCE LEE If you are talking about sport (boxing, for example) you have regulations and rules, but when you are talking about fighting, real fighting, there are no rules, so you better train every part of your body.

– The Pierre Berton Show, September 1971

SHANNON LEE Jeet Kune Do was developed as real street fighting. There are no illegal moves. It's about doing what you need to do to win; you can bite, you can gouge eyes, you can hit to the groin, you can do all that sort of stuff.

BRUCE LEE Martial art, like any art, is an expression of the human being. Some expressions have taste, some are logical (maybe under certain required situations), but most involve merely performing some sort of a mechanical repetition of a fixed pattern. This is most unhealthy because to live is to express, and to express you have to create. Creation is never something old, and definitely not merely repetition. Remember well, my friend, that all styles are man-made, and the man is always more

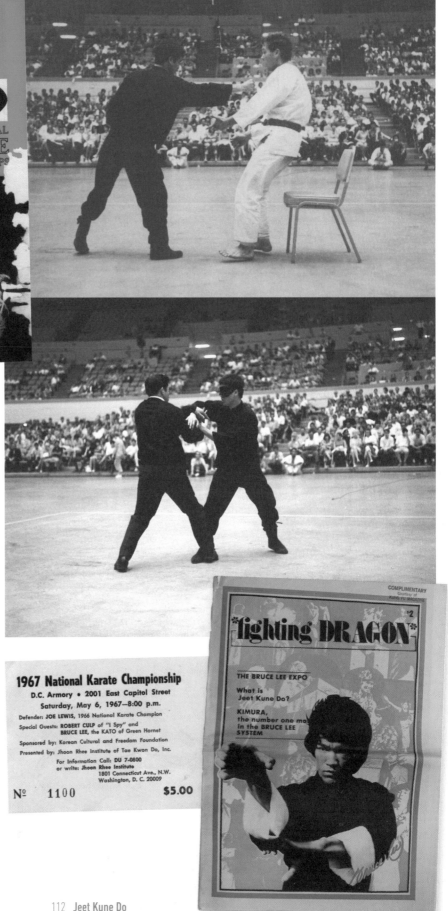

PROGRAM 50¢

1967 INTERNATIONAL KARATE CHAMPIONSHIPS

JAMES COBURN Bruce came over to the house and he was just bursting with energy. We were talking a little bit and he told me about a one inch punch that he said was better than anything I had done. I told him I'd like to see that. So I stood up, put a pillow in front of me and bang! He knocked me into the chair, the chair fell down and I rolled over to the corner with the one inch punch. I said, 'Let's go to work, that looks like fun.' I told him that he should get into films, he would achieve things. For the first couple he would learn things and he would eventually be the king of the heap. It certainly turned out that way. As Bruce would say, the only thing you have to overcome is yourself. The enemy is the self, not anybody outside. You find that person and you integrate yourself with it.

International Karate Championships, 1967
Bruce can be seen demonstrating the one inch punch (top right) and fighting while blindfolded (middle)

1967 National Karate Championship
D.C. Armory • 2001 East Capitol Street
Saturday, May 6, 1967—8:00 p.m.
Defender: JOE LEWIS, 1966 National Karate Champion
Special Guests: ROBERT CULP of "I Spy" and
BRUCE LEE, the KATO of Green Hornet
Sponsored by: Korean Cultural and Freedom Foundation
Presented by: Jhoon Rhee Institute of Tae Kwon Do, Inc.
For Information Call: DU 7-0800
or write: Jhoon Rhee Institute
1801 Connecticut Ave., N.W.
Washington, D. C. 20009
Nº 1100 $5.00

COMPLIMENTARY

fighting DRAGON #2

THE BRUCE LEE EXPO

What is
Jeet Kune Do?

KIMURA,
the number one ma
in the BRUCE LEE
SYSTEM

In the following years Bruce worked hard at furthering his acting career and did get roles in a few TV series and films, including *Marlowe* (1969) and *Longstreet* (1971). To support the family, Bruce taught private lessons in Jeet Kune Do, often to people in the entertainment industry, including Steve McQueen, James Coburn, Stirling Silliphant and Ted Ashley.

TAKY KIMURA He knew that if you were giving your best, he'd work with you. He tried to structure things in terms of your mentality and physical abilities and then he would tailor something that he knew you could handle.

1968

一九六八年

HOLLYWOOD 好莱坞

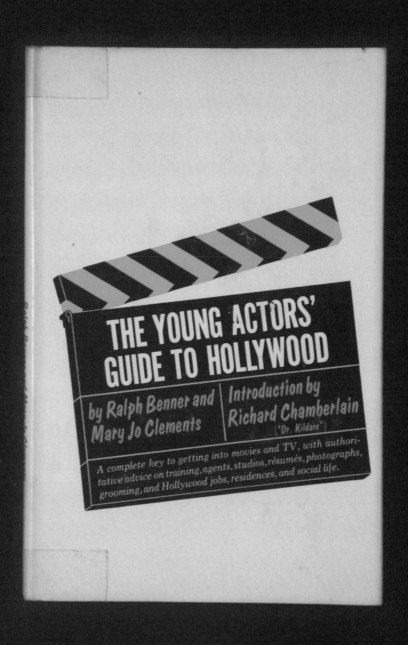

THE YOUNG ACTORS'
GUIDE TO HOLLYWOOD

by Ralph Benner and
Mary Jo Clements

Introduction by
Richard Chamberlain
("Dr. Kildare")

A complete key to getting into movies and TV, with authori-
tative advice on training, agents, studios, résumés, photographs,
grooming, and Hollywood jobs, residences, and social life.

BRUCE LEE
IN MY OWN PROCESS
LETTER EIGHT

It is easy to criticise and break down the spirit of others, but to know yourself takes maybe a lifetime. To take responsibility for one's actions, good and bad, is something else. After all, all knowledge simply means self-knowledge.

MCQUEEN
Aug. 23 (STEVE)
" 25 (")
" 28 (")
SEPT. 2
SEPT. 5
SEPT. 11
OCT. 17

Cash Account AUGUST   Received   Paid

Cash Account SEPTEMBER   Received   Paid

STEVE McQUEEN I met Bruce in Los Angeles in 1968 or '69. I'm not involved in the martial arts to any degree. I'm not an expert or anything like that. Bruce was just a personal friend of mine and I cared for him a lot.

Sometimes I'd feel rotten and the phone would ring, and it would be Bruce. I don't know why he called. He would just say, 'I just thought I should call you.'

I thought Bruce was a brilliant, fine philosopher about everyday living, and I was very taken with his theories and approach to the martial arts. He was very much into finding out who he was. His comment to people was, 'Know yourself.' Know yourself, I would imagine, through the martial arts, which was some type of an extension of himself. But he also knew himself in everyday life.

The good head that he acquired was good through his knowing himself. He and I used to have great long discussions about that. No matter what you do in life, if you don't know yourself, you're never going to be able to appreciate anything in life. That, I think, is today's mark of a good human being – to know yourself.

BRUCE LEE Steve McQueen is good in [the fighting] department because that son of a gun has got the toughness in him.

– *The Pierre Berton Show, September 1971*

Above right: Bruce with Steve McQueen and
Fumio Demura

2
TUES.
9:10 – 9:25   WARM UP
WAIST, LEG, STOMACH
9:27 – 9:41   RUN
11:30 – 12:35
   PUNCH – 500
   FINGER JAB – 400
3 PM – 3:45 – SQUAT
PUNCHING
   1) WEIGHT – 3 SETS
   2) LIGHT BAG – 20 MIN.
   3) HEAVY BAG – 3 SETS
(EMPHASIZING LEFT CROSS)
5:15 – 5:45 ~ SIT UPS – 5 SETS
     SIDE BENDS – 5 SETS
     LEG RAISES – 5 SETS
8:20 – (4 min) FOREARM ISOM.

TOTAL : 2 HRS. 53 MIN.

CHUCK CALLED
(BLISTER ON FIST) NIGHT

Gung Fu workout – 7 – 9 PM.
sticking Hand (All Present)
3
WED.
9:00 – 9:15
   WARM-UP – WAIST, LEG, STOMACH
9:20 – 9:50
   PUNCH (BACK FIST) 500
   SKIP ROPE ~ 3 SETS
10:00 – 10:30
   FINGER JAB (500)
11:05 – 11:15   RUN
3:05 – 4:00
1) HIGH KICK STRETCHING (L&R) 4 SETS
2) SIDE LEG "   (L & R) 4 SETS
3) PULLY HIP EXTENSION – 3 SETS
4) RT. LEADING HOOK KICK
   1) heavy bag – 3 SETS
   2) paper – 3 SETS
5) Rear left hook kick
   1) heavy bag – 3 SETS
4:15 – 4:35   2) paper – 3 SETS
STOMACH – WAIST – 3 & 4 of 4 SETS
   FOREARM ISOMETRIC

18
THUR.
11 a m – 12:40
   – STOMACH
1) SIT UP – 5 SETS
2) SIDE BENDS – 5 SETS
3) LEG RAISES – 5 SETS
   SKIPPING ROPE – 5 SETS
LIGHT BAG – ONE–TWO 3 SETS
HEAVY BAG – OVERHAND 3 SETS
3:20 – ONE-LEGGED SQUAT 2 SETS
FOREARM/WRIST ISOMETRIC
STANCE / SQUAT ISOMETRIC

3:45 – RUNNING (2)

(rest knuckles for one day)

— 黐手 —

5:30 – DINNER – THE GEE

[Gung Fu workout]

11:00 – PUNCH – 500
19
FRI.
12:00 — 2:30
16 黐手 ~ CHUCK NORRIS

9 P.M – STOMACH : —
   SIDE BENDS — 5 SETS
   LEG RAISES — 5 SETS
   SIT – UP — 5 SETS

FOREARM/WRIST ISOMETRIC
STANCE/ SQUAT ISOMETRIC
   ONE-LEGGED SQUAT – 2 SETS
LEG STRETCHING : —
   STAND —
   1) straight
   2) side
   3) knee out
PUNCH SUPPLEMENT – 500
   TOTAL — 1,000 punch
(blister on second knuckle

1968 planner detailing workout regime

MARLOWE
Detective muy privado

BRUCE LEE · CARROLL O'CONNOR · RITA MORENO

director PAUL BOGART
METROCOLOR

DIRECTOR Paul Bogart
WRITER Stirling Silliphant
PRODUCERS Sidney Beckerman, Gabriel Katzka

JAMES GARNER as Philip Marlowe
GAYLE HUNNICUTT as Mavis Wald
BRUCE LEE as Winslow Wong
CARROLL O'CONNOR as Lt. Christy French
RITA MORENO as Dolores Gonzáles

RELEASE DATE 22 October 1969 (US)

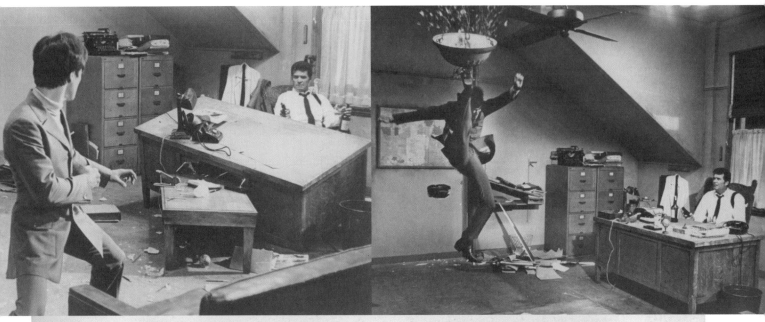

1872-27

HOW TO GET A KICK OUT OF LIFE....James Garner finds himself
faced with a high stepper in this sequence from MGM's "The
Little Sister", in which Bruce Lee of the underworld shows
how foot work can get you ahead.

RANDALL PARK As an Asian American, I grew up obsessed with Bruce Lee, as many kids were. When I was growing up there were only a handful of recognisable Asian faces on TV and film that I feel represented me. One of them was Pat Morita, who I'd seen on shows like *Happy Days* and *Sanford and Son*. It was one of the few times I saw an Asian American on screen, playing an Asian American, speaking without an accent and just kind of hanging out, making jokes with his friends. The characters Pat played were very relatable but not necessarily aspirational, like Bruce Lee was. Bruce was someone who I wanted to be – a real hero, badass, confident and handsome.

TED WONG He was able to express himself and had such a magnetism. I think that what he was doing in the movies became a standard.

Action scenes from *Marlowe*, 1968

RANDALL PARK As I got older, I read more about him, learned more about him and just became so captivated by him. To see someone so fully self-actualised – you can't deny that. It's just so mesmerising. To be yourself is a simple idea but it's not always easy to do in this world, and as I got older I realised that was what was so captivating about him. Number one, he was an Asian person, which I didn't see a lot of growing up, so that was interesting to me, but then to also see someone who was so wholly himself was what really resonated, not just with this community but everybody globally.

It doesn't mean that he was a perfect person because there's no such thing. That also resonates because I can still aspire to this level of self-actualisation without worrying about always being perfect and knowing exactly what to say. No, I'm human. You can still aspire and work on oneself. It's a process, which is really cool.

TED WONG In the movies, he made [the moves] more flashy to make it more exciting. Some of the techniques he used in the movies were definitely not used in the real fighting. In his own martial art, his technique would have been more compact and simple and direct. Everything to the point.

DIRECTOR Phil Karlson
WRITER William McGivern
PRODUCER Irving Allen
TECHNICAL DIRECTOR Bruce Lee

DEAN MARTIN as Matt Helm
ELKE SOMMER as Linda Karensky
SHARON TATE as Freya Carlson
NANCY KWAN as Wen Yurang
NIGEL GREEN as Count Contini

RELEASE DATE 5 February 1969 (US)

Bruce rehearsing moves with Dean Martin

NANCY KWAN Bruce and I got to know each other working on *The Wrecking Crew*. He was the karate advisor on the film. I remember him telling me, 'Nancy, I'm going to go back to Hong Kong and become a big martial arts star!' Bruce was full of energy. I believed him and that's what he did – he went back to Hong Kong and he became a big martial arts star.

Top: Bruce with Sharon Tate and Nancy Kwan
Above: Bruce and Nancy Kwan

RANDALL PARK In my opinion, a good director has a vision. A good director is able to work with others to get that vision realised while also being open-minded enough to consider the input of others and find ways to make the original vision even better, more full, more alive. A good director should be able to work with every kind of person in every kind of situation and can keep cool in challenging times. A good director is a good leader.

Top left: Bruce and Dean Martin
Top right and middle: Bruce and Sharon Tate
Left: *The Wrecking Crew* crew – Ed Parker, Joe Lewis, Dean Martin, Bruce, Mike Stone

我的明確目標 1969–1970

一九六九年——一九七零年

MY DEFINITE CHIEF AIM

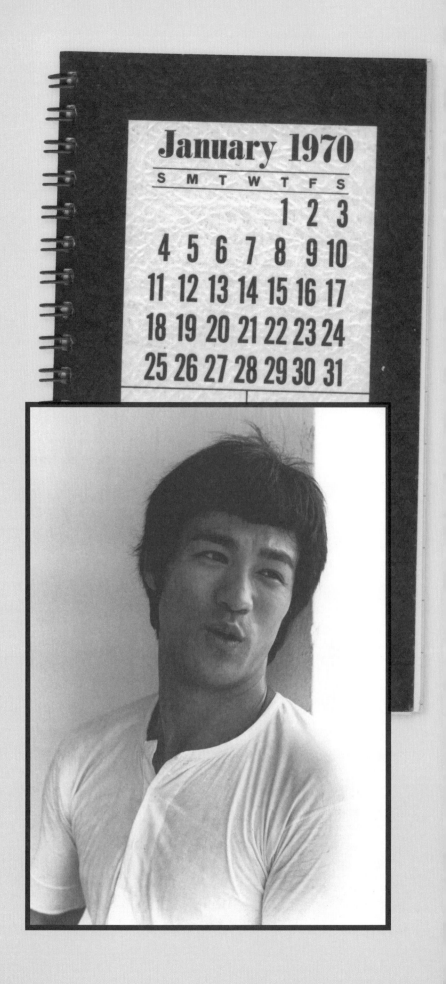

January 1970

S	M	T	W	T	F	S
				1	2	3
4	5	6	7	8	9	10
11	12	13	14	15	16	17
18	19	20	21	22	23	24
25	26	27	28	29	30	31

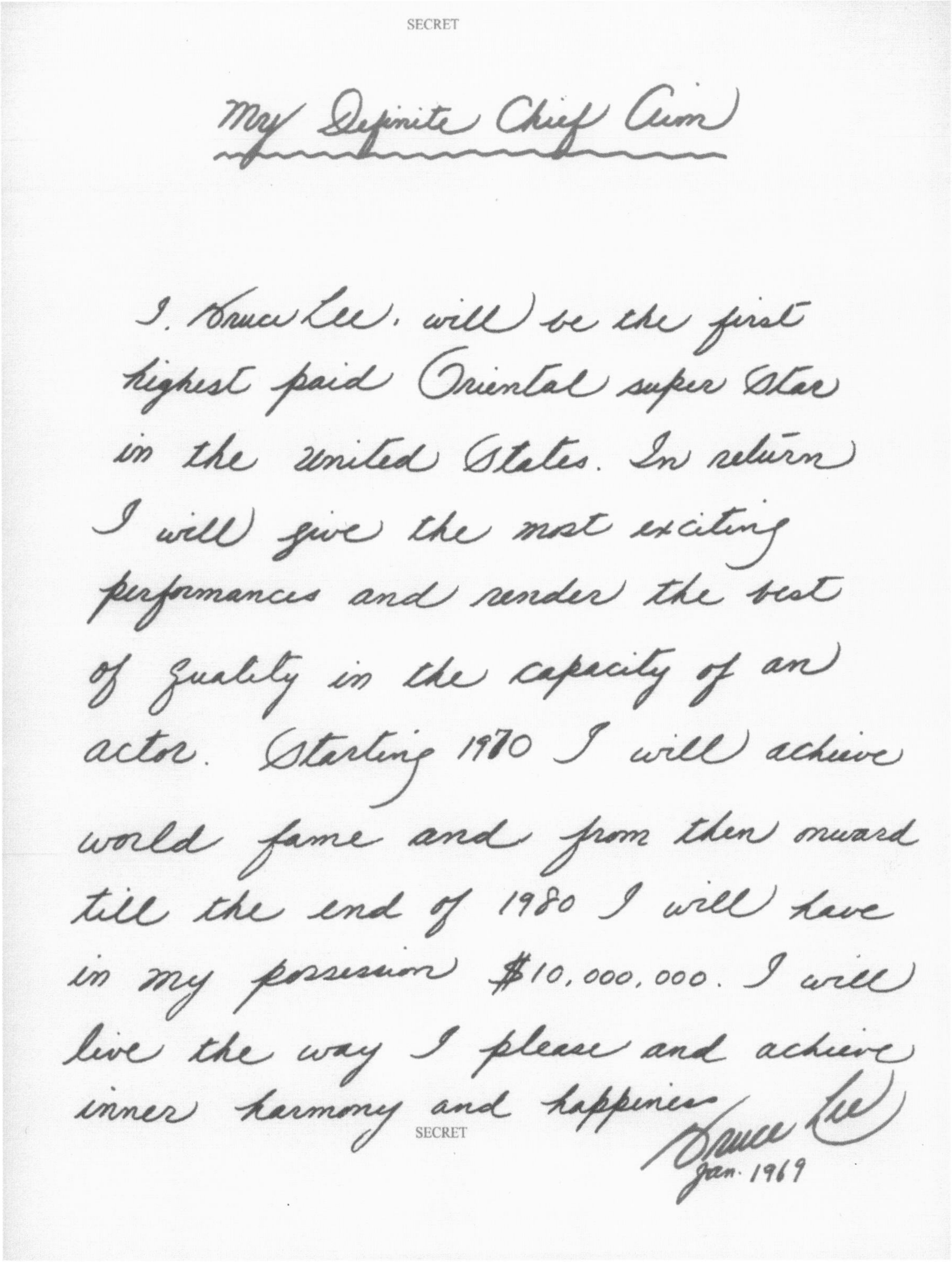

My Definite Chief Aim

I, Bruce Lee, will be the first highest paid Oriental super Star in the United States. In return I will give the most exciting performances and render the best of quality in the capacity of an actor. Starting 1970 I will achieve world fame and from then onward till the end of 1980 I will have in my possession $10,000,000. I will live the way I please and achieve inner harmony and happiness

Bruce Lee
Jan. 1969

BRUCE LEE
IN MY OWN PROCESS
LETTER FIVE

When another human being sees a self-actualising person walk past, he cannot help but say, 'Hey, now there is someone real!'

In January 1969, Bruce Lee wrote down his 'Definite Chief Aim' – his personal ambition to become the biggest Asian actor in Hollywood

BRUCE LEE I think it's important in the United States that the oriental, the true oriental, should be shown. In Hollywood its always the pigtail and bouncing around with the eyes slanted, which is very out of date.

– *The Pierre Berton Show, September 1971*

1969 JANUARY

encourage my conscience
to guide me as to what
is right and what is
wrong, but I will never
set aside the verdict it
renders, no matter what
may be the cost of
carrying them out.

Bruce Lee

發則處於憂患、
失則處於安樂

1 New Year's Day

Wed. Things live by mov-
ing, and gain strength
as they go.

201 - AMOUNT $30 · BOOKS

JANUARY 1969

William Roger
Ingle
51T W. A+ G240342   **2** Thur.

765-8716

Competition motor   **3**
                           Fri.
883-6600

Joe Lewis:—
            826-3120

Joe Bodner - 838-6587   **4**
Joe Hyams - 274-6440
            278-456 Sat.

Memo.

KAREEM ABDUL-JABBAR He was playful but he loved the martial arts and he didn't want to see it be abused. It wasn't about chopsocky, he had nothing to do with that.

JEFF CHANG When Bruce moved to the US the civil rights movement was underway. It was a period of upheaval that he was living through, and he happened to be the person in the right place and time to carry forward some of the breakthroughs of those social movements for justice into the global culture. He was able to embody the aspirations of people who wanted freedom and who were rising up all around the world in the late 1960s, early 1970s. I think that makes him a revolutionary symbol even though he was never explicitly politically involved.

Bruce Lee

BRUCE LEE

(1/7/1969)

SECRET

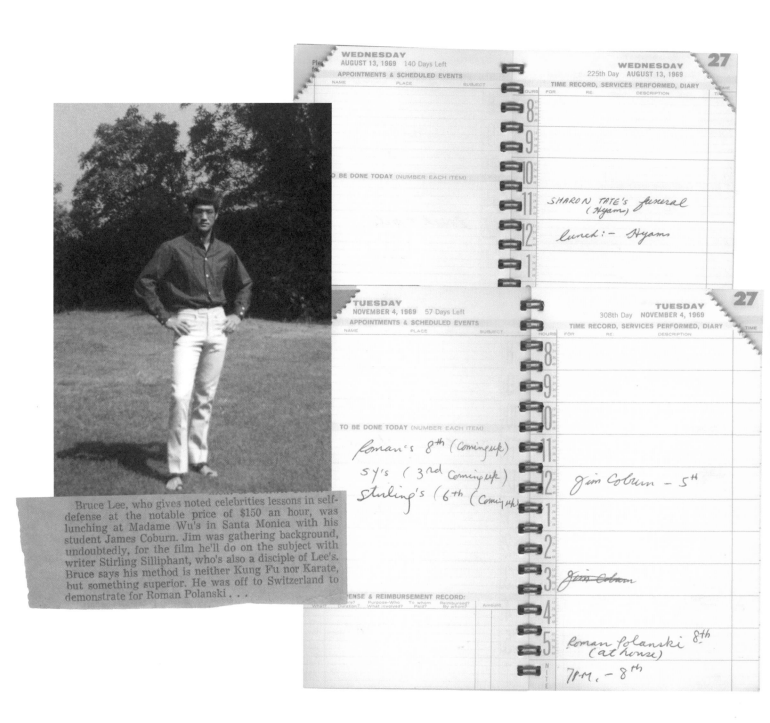

BRUCE LEE Just what is an actor? Is he not the sum total of all understanding, his capability to captivate the audience because he is real in the expression of his personal feelings towards what is required by the scene. You can spot such artists from ordinary ones like that. The American has a word for it, it's called 'charisma'. What you see on the screen is the sum total of his level of understanding, his taste, his educational background, his intensity, and so forth, and so on.

– Notes titled 'Self-Actualization and Self-Image: Actualization in the Art of Acting'

1969 planner detailing Sharon Tate's funeral
and meetings with Roman Polanski and
Stirling Silliphant

SHANNON LEE He loved his Chinese culture but rather than shielding it and keeping it to himself, he wanted to share it and share it authentically. That is why he decided to develop a path in films and TV; it was an opportunity for him to share his culture and an authentic representation of himself as a Chinese man via a bigger medium than his schools.

October 26 (Sunday) 1969
(MGM TOUR)
Washington D.C.
Jhoon Rhee's home

Jan. 7th — make up mind to make goal

Jan. 13th — convince stirling on project

Jan. 14th — convince Coburn on taking part

Jan. 20th — ① MEETING :- stirling, Jim, me, Mark

FEB. 28th — second meeting

APRIL 18 — meeting-stirling Tense.

MAY 12 — meeting-Coburn New York

MAY 27 — meeting-Coburn, Stirling, mark.

Sept. 1st — stirling, Jim, burton.

JANUARY 1969

FIX GARAGE DOOR

STEVE CALLED

STUDY

12 noon — stirling lunch

FORMATION OF STIRLING AND ME ON MOVIE IDEA

CALL JAMES

STUDY

① 3PM. JAMES COBURN

BURNS INVOLMENT

dinner & movie Jim & Beverly

11:30 — Peter Lunch

stop by Little Joe (a trim)

— Peter, Ted

UV — 15 MIN.

JANUARY 1969

STIRLING'S BIRTHDAY **16**

② 3PM. James Coburn Thur.

Herb over

STUDY

UV — 15 MIN. **17**

STUDY Fri.

Columbia "Wrecking Crew" screening 17th Studio Rm. 7 – 4PM

Talk to Stirling

— STUDY — **18**

Dan's over 1:30 Sat.

Memo.

KEEP YOUR MIND ON THE THINGS YOU WANT AND OFF THE THINGS YOU DON'T WANT

"ATTITUDE"

BRUCE LEE We had a meeting on Project 'Leng' last Friday, James Coburn, Stirling Silliphant and I. Project 'Leng' is a code name for our martial arts motion picture. 'Leng' is a Chinese word meaning beautiful. James Coburn is a very peaceful man. He learned martial arts because it is like a mirror to reflect himself.

– *Letter to Grandmaster Jhoon Rhee, March 1969*

Top: 1969 day planner detailing meetings with Stirling Silliphant and James Coburn
Above and opposite: Bruce and James Coburn

PINGREE-PANPIPER PRODUCTIONS

present

a

film

by

James Coburn   Bruce Lee   Stirling Silliphant

"THE SILENT FLUTE"

Written

by

Stirling Silliphant

FIRST DRAFT
March 27, 1973

MB-1

JAMES COBURN Bruce and I were working out and we started talking about the possibilities of some kind of film. We just started talking about the outline, about a guy whose yoga is martial arts, and there's a book – there had to be an aim: the achievement of finding the book – and the keeper of this book is this great martial artist. The guy has to go through all these trials, which we invented. It was sort of a lot of Sufi tales interspersed with a few Zen ideas. We all contributed to it. We'd go in and work two hours, three days a week at Stirling's office and we'd take notes and we evolved the thing in about six weeks.

Above: Script for the film *The Silent Flute*, which was made in 1978 as *Circle of Iron*. Script meetings began in 1969 and continued for four years. After Bruce's death in 1973, Silliphant and Stanley Mann completed the screenplay
Right: Bruce and screenwriter Stirling Silliphant

BLINDMAN, PLAY A QUIET SONG

In the awakening purple of dawn, barely visible in the distance, the small image of a man is (briskly) ascending the misty mountain. The silence of the morning is punctuated with the humble sound of one distant flute; the marriage of tranquil elements on a seemingly virgin morning.

The man walks higher and higher up the incline, as the sun rises like a great slow bubble of air through water toward a higher skin of surface. The increasing light, and a closer glimpse, reveals the identity of the climbing man, JAMES COBURN, as he walks still higher with hurried purposeful strides.

Now the sun is bright in the sky. Over COBURN's shoulder is seen another figure - that of a man playing the flute, sitting on a large rock.

The two men consider each other's presence, saying nothing. The fluteplayer puts his flute away and stands. COBURN and the fluteplayer face each other from opposite ends of the wide screen. Then, with screams of oriental fury, they rush towards each other, as if in attack.

Jumping back in time, the events leading up to this moment will unfold.

*   *   *   *

The intense noise and staccato violence of the world's championship freeform martial arts contest sharply contrasts with the

-1-

BRUCE LEE Basically this is a story of one man's quest for his liberation, the returning to his original sense of freedom. Unlike the old West's 'fastest gun alive', the individual is not out to sharpen his tools to destroy his antagonist; rather, his side kick, back fist, hook kick, and so forth, are directed primarily towards himself.

– *Silent Flute* notes, May 1970

The Silent Flute plot summary

JAMES COBURN We had a really great time in India. Stirling, Bruce and I travelled around looking for the wilderness. We went to Rajasthan, which was great, and we saw the desert there but we didn't find the wilderness. I took some great shots of Bruce doing some flying kicks off a sand dune. He was soaring, it was great. We spent, I guess, about four days in Rajasthan. We had a meeting with the Maharajah of Bikaner and the three of us had dinner with him that night right on the edge of the desert. He was a member of parliament there, he showed us around. We found some wonderful places, but we didn't really find any place we could shoot.

James Coburn and Bruce's visit
to Rajasthan, India, in search of filiming
locations, February 1971

PRODUCTION BUDGET
CAST

Production No.
Production *THE SILENT FLUTE*

SHEET NO. 1

CHARACTER	ARTIST	RATE PER WEEK	START	CLOSE	WEEKS	GUARANTEE WEEKS	CHARACTER EXPIRATION DATE (EST)	AMOUNT
COKO	James Coburn							75,000
DR. SAHM								
CHANSHA								50,000
MONKEY MAN	Bruce Lee							
PANTHER MAN								
SHABANI								
TARA								25,000
YAMAGUCHI								
MECHANICAL MAN								
Balance of Cast and Bits								35,000

TOTAL 210,000

Account No. 110 — CAST						SUMMARY		
ACC'T. NO.						ACC'T NO.		
110-01	Contract Players					110-04	Stock Players	
-01	Allowance For Looping					110-05	Borrowed Players	
10-02	Free Lance Players					-05	Allowance For Looping	
-02	Allowance For Looping					110-09	Cast Overtime	
110-03	Day Rates – Sheet No. 2					110-10	Cost Living Allowance	
-03	Day Rates – Sheet No. 3						TOTAL 110	210,000

BRUCE LEE It is because of the self that there arises the foe. When there are no signs (or thought movements) stirred in your mind, no conflicts of opposition take place there; and where there are no conflicts (of one trying to 'get the better' of the other), this is known as 'neither self nor foe'. At their best, the 'tools' thus represent the force of intuitive or instinctive directness, which, unlike the intellect, does not divide itself, blocking its own passageway. It marches onward without looking forward or sideways.

The basic problem of a martial artist is known as 'psychical stoppage'. This occurs when he is engaged in a deadly contest with his antagonist, and his mind attaches itself to thoughts or any object it encounters. Unlike the fluid mind in everyday life, his mind is 'stopped'. Incapable of flowing from one object to another without stickiness or clogginess. At this point, the martial artist ceases to be master of himself, and, as a result, his tools no longer express themselves in their suchness. So, to have something in one's mind means that it is preoccupied and has no time for anything else; however, to attempt to remove the thought already in it is to refill it with another something!

– *Silent Flute notes, May 1970*

Top: Bruce, Stirling Silliphant, James Coburn
and producer Yash Johar, Rajasthan, India, 1971
Above: Budget sheet for *The Silent Flute*

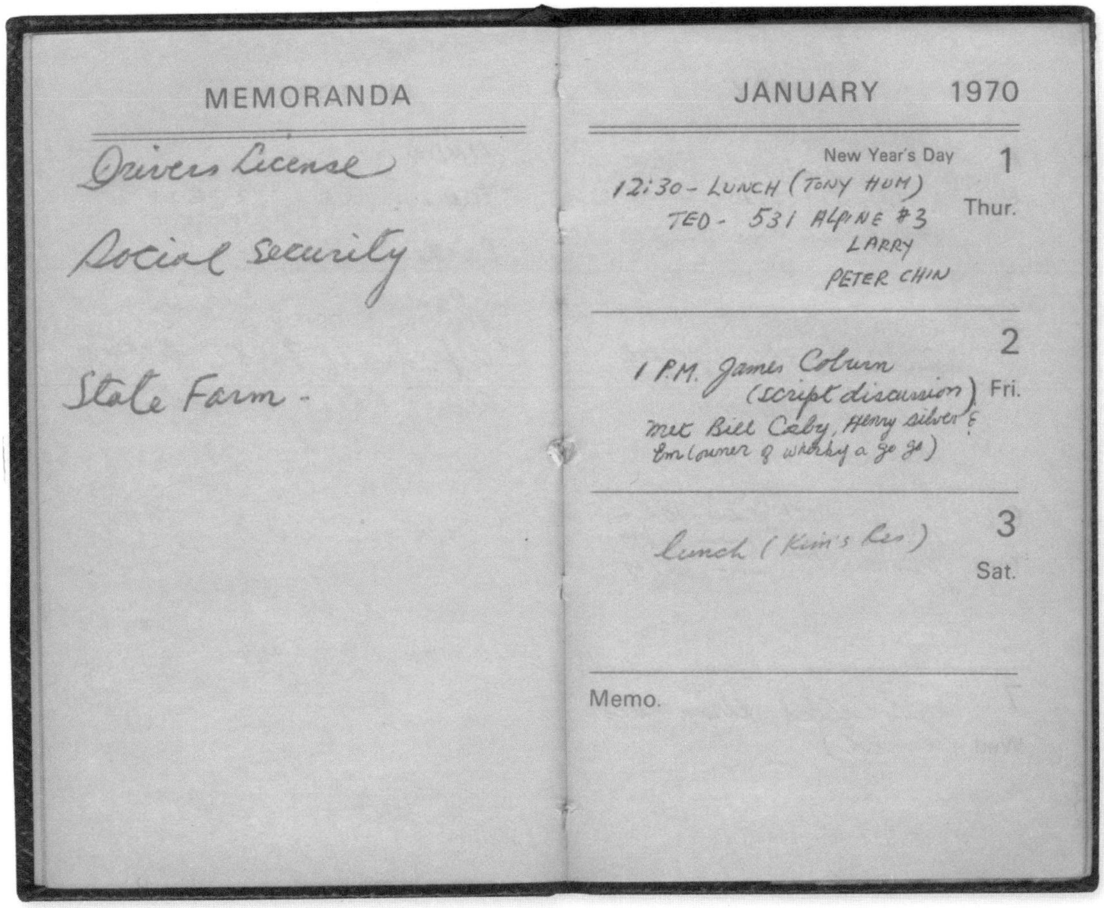

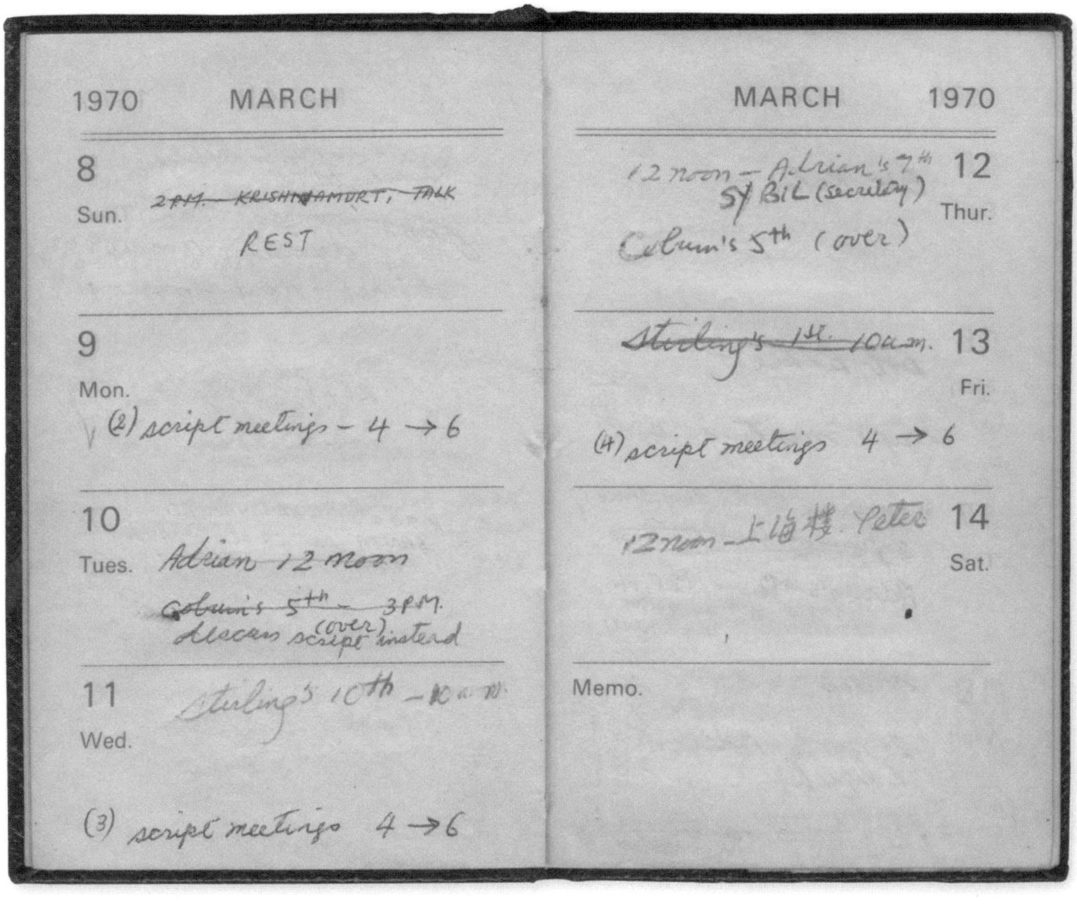

MEMORANDA

Drivers License

Social Security

State Farm -

JANUARY 1970

1 New Year's Day
Thur.
12:30 - LUNCH (TONY HUM)
TED - 531 ALPINE #3
LARRY
PETER CHIN

2
Fri.
1 P.M. James Colburn
(script discussion)
met Bill Coby, Henry silver &
Em Louner & whitey a go go?)

3
Sat.
lunch (Kim's Res.)

Memo.

1970 MARCH

8
Sun.
2PM KRISHNAMURTI, TALK
REST

9
Mon.
√ (2) script meetings - 4 → 6

10
Tues.
Adrian 12 noon
Colburn's 5th 3 P.M.
(over)
discuss script instead

11
Wed.
Sterling's 10th - 10 a.m.

(3) script meetings 4 → 6

MARCH 1970

12
Thur.
12 noon - Adrian's 7th
SY BIL (secretary)
Colburn's 5th (over)

13
Fri.
Sterling's 1st 10 a.m.

(4) script meetings 4 → 6

14
Sat.
12 noon - 上海樓. Peter

Memo.

1970 day planner detailing script meetings for
The Silent Flute

Name	No.
Leo Alcindor	
Mito Uyehara	
Black Belt Mag.	WE8-234.

WILL POWER :—

Recognizing that the power of will is the supreme Court over all other departments of my mind, I will exercise it daily, when I need the urge to action for any purpose; and I will form habit designed to bring the power of my will into action at least once daily.

Emotion :—

Realizing that my emotions are both POSITIVE and negative I will form daily HABITS which I will encourage the development of the POSITIVE EMOTIONS, and aid me in Converting the negative emotions into some form of useful action.

Reason :—

Recognizing that both my positive and negative emotions may be dangerous if they are not controlled and guided to desirable ends, I will

FINISHED FILES ARE THE RESULT OF SCIENTIFIC STUDY COMBINED WITH EXPERIENCE OF YEARS

WILL POWER

Recognizing that the power of will is the supreme Court over all other departments of my mind, I will exercise it daily, when I need the urge to action for any purpose; and I will form HABIT designed to bring the power of my will into action at least once daily.

EMOTION

Realizing that my emotions are both POSITIVE and negative I will form daily HABITS which will ENCOURAGE the development of the POSITIVE EMOTIONS, and aid me in Converting the negative emotions into some form of useful action.

REASON

Recognizing that both my positive and negative emotions may be dangerous if they are not controlled and guided to desirable ends, I will submit all my desires, aims, and purposes to my faculty of reason, and I will be guided by it in giving expression to these.

IMAGINATION

Recognizing the need for sound plans and ideas for the attainment of my desires, I will develop my imagination by calling upon it daily for help in the formation of my plans sumit all my desires, aims, and purposes to my faculty of reason, and I will be guided by it in giving expression to these.

Imagination:—

Recognizing the need for sound plans and ideas for the attainment of my desires, I will develop my imagination by calling upon it daily for help in the formation of my plans.

Memory:—

Recognizing the value of an alert mind and an alert memory, I will encourage mine to become alert by taking care to impress it clearly with all thoughts I wish to recall, and by associating those thoughts with related subjects which I may call to mind frequently.

Subconscious Mind:—

Recognizing the influence of my subconscious mind over my power of will, I shall take care to submit to it a clear and definite picture of my MAJOR PURPOSE in life and all minor purposes leading to my major purpose, and I shall keep this picture CONSTANTLY BEFORE MY SUBCONSCIOUS MIND BY REPEATING IT DAILY.

Conscience:—

Recognizing that my emotions often err in their over-enthusiasm, and my faculty of reason often is without the warmth of feeling that is necessary to enable me to combine justice with mercy in my judgements, I will

BRUCE LEE Ultimately, one should be 'purposeless'. By 'purposeless' is not meant mere absence of things where vacant nothingness prevails. The object is not to be stuck with thought process. The spirit is by nature formless, and no 'objects' are to be stuck in it.

– *Silent Flute notes, May 1970*

KAREEM ABDUL-JABBAR To be like water you have to be able to adapt. You have to understand that not every road is straight, that there are some huge puddles and even bridges missing, but you have to accept that and deal with the unexpected. I think that's what Bruce was all about – understanding that it doesn't always go the way you want it to go, but knowing that if you can adapt you can prevail.

Bruce's affirmations in pocket notebooks and a loose page, 1969

1 You will never get any more out of this life than you expect

Keep your mind on the things you want and off those you don't

Things live by moving and gain strength as they go

Be a calm beholder of whats happening around you

There is a difference :- (a) the world (2) our reaction of it

be aware of our conditioning drop & dissolve inner blockage

we start by dissolving our attitude, not by trying to alter outer condition — inner to outer

see that there is no one to fight only an illusion to see through

no one can hurt you unless you allow him to

Inwardly, psychologically, be a nobody.

DAY	START	STOP	MILES	TOLLS & PARKING	MISC.
1					
2					
3					
4					
5					
6					
7					
8					
9					
10					
11					
12					
13					
14					
15					
16					
17					
18					
19					
20					
21					
22					
23					
24					
25					
26					
27					
28					
29					
30					
31					
TOTALS					

POCKET DAY-
Allentown, Pa.

I know that I have the ability to ACHIEVE the object of my DEFINITE PURPOSE in life; therefore, I DEMAND of myself persistent CONTINUOUS action toward its attainment, and I here and now promise to render such action.

I realize the DOMINATING THOUGHTS of my mind will eventually reproduce themselves in outward, physical action, and gradually transform themselves into physical reality; therefore I will CONCENTRATE my thoughts for 30 min. daily upon the task of thinking of the person I intend to become, thereby creating in my mind a clear MENTAL PICTURE.

I know through the principle of autosuggestion, any desire that I PERSISTENTLY hold in my mind will eventually seek expression through some practical means of attaining the object back of it; therefore I will devote 10 min. daily to DEMANDING of myself the development of SELF-CONFIDENCE.

STEVE AOKI The easiest philosophy for me to remember is 'be like water'. The other one that applies to my life is 'sometimes a goal is just something to aim at'. It's more about the journey than the goal and that applies to my start-ups, like my record label Dim Mak, which I named because of my fascination with Bruce Lee. I wanted to come up with something clever and there's this whole mystery of the Dim Mak (a legendary touch of death) and Bruce Lee. So every time I would start something it wasn't like, 'What is my five-year plan?' I might have it but I will follow my inspirations and passions and that might get me somewhere else and I will just go with that journey.

Affirmations, 1969

(1). ~~Copy~~ buddhist script. — (takes several
    month — but 3 days did)
    (sneaky because hard work)

(2). old man like sculpturing.
    ———— because of "simplicity"
    Also, Art is life and not only
    limiting to martial art.

(3).

BRUCE LEE Where the energy is tipped, there is too much of it in one direction, while in another there is a shortage. Where there is too much, it overflows and cannot be controlled; where there is a shortage, it is not sufficiently nourished and shrivels up. In both cases, it is unable to cope with ever-changing situations.

But when there prevails a state of 'purposelessness' (which is also a state of fluidity, empty-mindedness, or simply the everyday mind), the spirit harbours nothing in it, nor is it tipped in any one direction; it transcends both subject and object; it responds empty-mindedly to environmental changes and leaves no track. In Chuang-tzu's words: 'The perfect man employs his mind as a mirror. It grasps nothing, yet it refuses nothing; it receives, but does not keep.' Like water filling a pond, which is always ready to flow off again, the spirit can work its inexhaustible power because it is free and is open to everything because it is empty.

– *Silent Flute notes, May 1970*

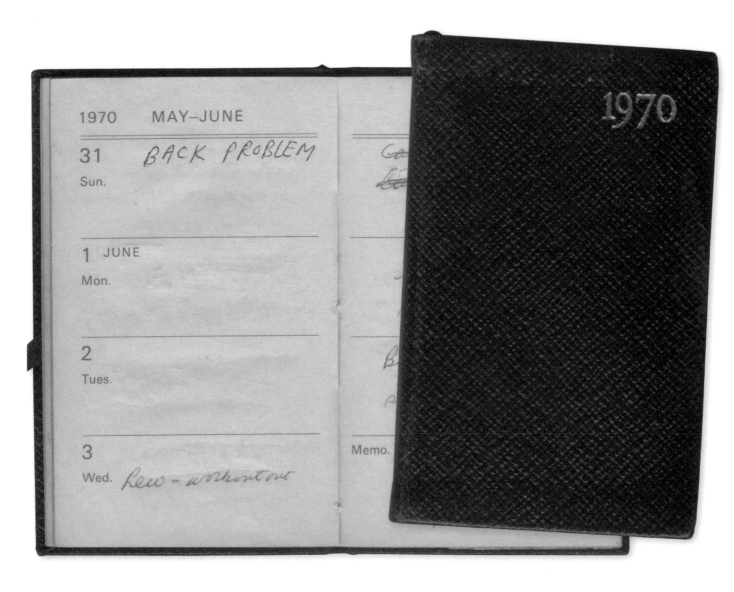

1970 MAY–JUNE

31 Sun. BACK PROBLEM

1 JUNE Mon.

2 Tues.

3 Wed. *Rew - workout out*

Memo.

LINDA LEE CADWELL At the moment that Bruce hurt his back it wasn't critical; it wasn't like he fell down on the floor in pain or anything like that. It was just like, 'Oh, that doesn't feel too good.' And then it came on more gradually after that. At first it wasn't like that was going to be the end of his career, right here, right now. No speeding off to the hospital. The pain just increased and increased until he sought some help with it and had x-rays. We had our family doctor and he sent him to orthopaedics and it then became a process of what was wrong and what should we do about it and would he consider surgery? Back pain is not something that is easily solved and there are often many options and back surgery even today is not a popular choice. It has consequences and so surgery was to be avoided and the prescription was rest. That became very difficult for him. However, he switched gears and said, 'Well, this is the time of my life when I'm going to do what I said I wanted to do and I'm going to start taking notes and reading, applying the things that I've learned to my life, to my martial arts, my philosophy.' And thus we have those volumes of writings that he did during that time – commentaries on the martial way. It was a down time, but he still found a way to be productive.

1970 diary noting Bruce's back injury which forced him to spend the next six months recuperating at home

BRUCE LEE To begin with, this article is not an easy one because it is most difficult to write about oneself, because each of us is such a complexity. It is similar to an eye that can see externally but not internally. Granted, it would be a much easier job if one happened to be the type who can indulge oneself in a manipulative game of an imaginative self. But this bothers me.

I have come to the realisation that sooner or later what it really amounts to is the bare fact that even an attempt to really write something about oneself demands, first of all, an honesty towards oneself, to be able to take responsibility to be what we actually are: that is, a pure human being.

– In My Own Process, Letter One

LINDA LEE CADWELL It was really a very difficult time and if there was ever a low moment in his lifetime that would be it. He was so discouraged and doctors were telling him that he had great reason to be discouraged because he was never going to be normal again. Normal as in walking, not to even speak of doing gung fu and kicks and stuff like that. So, when the experts are telling you that, that's just a very, very low time. He just had to get through it. He had to lie low, take care of his back and allow it to heal. But he just started figuring it out for himself in addition to taking the doctors' advice. He would get books on kinesiology, on therapy.

FF-A-7

BRUCE LEE Having gone through a lot of these ups and downs, I realise that there is no help but self-help. Self-help comes in many forms: daily discoveries through choiceless observation, honestly, as well as wholeheartedly, always doing one's best; a sort of indomitable, obsessive dedication; and, above all, realising that there is no end or limit to this, because life is simply an ever-going process, an ever-renewing process. The duty of a human being, in my personal opinion, is to become transparently real, to simply be.

– In My Own Process, Letter One

The note in the image reads:
HELLO BRANDON! WHEN I COME BACK WE WILL GO TO THE TOY SHOP. LOVE YOU MY SON DAD P.S. WILL YOU KISS MAMA AND SHANNON FOR ME!?

LINDA LEE CADWELL He laid out a programme for himself from his readings because the doctors told him not even to walk at first. So he didn't at first. He could get up to walk to the bathroom and stuff but basically he stayed flat, using ice, painkillers. Then he followed a step-by-step process from his readings, very gradually. First walking a little bit, then a little faster, getting on his bike, which was great therapy.

It was a team effort. Brandon and Shannon were there too, which you might think would be difficult, but actually was very helpful to Bruce. They learned that they couldn't jump up and down on the bed, but it was a delight to him to have Shannon crawl up on the bed, have Brandon sitting next to him. We both read to the kids all of the time and that was a way he could participate with the children. It was a time of closeness.

SHANNON LEE My father died when I was four, so my memories are very brief, more like glimpses or quick snapshots. But the strongest and most profound memory that I have of him is what he felt like to me and how he made me feel. If you think about those years from birth to four, you are primarily taking in your world through your senses since you are pre-verbal for a good portion of that time. You're just feeling everything. For the longest time I would say to myself, 'Why do I feel like I know him so personally and so intimately?' I couldn't understand it. But later I came to realise, I knew him so essentially because he was so present, so real and so engaged with me. I knew, for lack of a better term, his soul. It was this way with so many other people as well. To this day, his closest friends and students throughout their whole lives would be moved to tears when they would talk about him. For me, I always held a deep love for him in my heart because he was my father, of course, but it was in discovering his writings as a young adult, while I was going through my own tough times surrounding my brother's death, that he started to really resonate with me on a profound level.

Above left: Linda at home with Brandon
Above right: Bruce training Brandon at Linda Palmer's home

In my own Process.   *By Bruce Lee*

my attempt to write a somewhat meaningful article — or else why write it at all — on how I, Bruce Lee by name, emotionally feel or how my instinctive honest reaction toward circumstances is no easy task. Why? Because I am a changing as well as an ever-growing man. thus what I hold true a couple of month ago might not the same now.

BRUCE LEE I don't know what I will be writing but just simply writing whatever wants to be written. If the writing communicates and stirs something within someone, it's beautiful. If not, well it can't be helped. Among people, great majorities don't feel comfortable at all with the unknown, that is, anything foreign that threatens their protected daily mould. So for the sake of their sense of security they construct chosen patterns, which they can justify.

Granted, unlike the lower animals, human beings are indeed intelligent beings. To be a martial artist means and demands absence of prejudice, superstition, ignorance, and all that – the primary, essential ingredient of what a quality fighter is, and leave the circus acts to the circus performers. Mentally, it means a burning enthusiasm with neutrality to choose to be.

– In My Own Process, Letter Two

LINDA LEE CADWELL It was a time for him to reflect about who he was and where he wanted to go. And, of course, that was the problem: where he wanted to go, that's where they were telling him he could not and he would not. Obviously, he did recover to an extent, where he did eventually do all of his gung fu and all the stunts that you see in the movies, but he was never free of back pain again in his lifetime. It was always something for which he needed therapy, either from me or a professional. When he was making his films in Hong Kong, they were so gruelling with all those fight scenes. I don't know how he could do that. He would come home every evening so sore and would have to have a massage or acupuncture or cupping. He did all kinds of therapy – you name it, he did it. It became a constant thing in his life.

SHANNON LEE That recovery and rehabilitation time expanded his consciousness and the vastness of his knowledge. Not only did he learn so intimately about his own anatomy and how to care for it, but he read a vast number of self-help books and created so many of his own writings then.

LINDA LEE CADWELL He became even more intense about his film career and his film future. He had always planned that he would not continue to do these heavy-duty action films forever. That was how he was breaking into the business. Just like the script for *The Silent Flute* was not heavy-duty action. That was the direction he was moving. He became even more deep thinking about his future and what he wanted to do. He had so many ideas and he was always jotting down things. I don't think he changed that much from how he was before the injury but maybe he was in more of a hurry. He wanted to do things right now.

1970	SEPTEMBER		SEPTEMBER	1970
6 Sun.			WALK	**10** Thur.
7 Labor Day Mon.	WALK		WALK	**11** Fri.
8 Tues.	WALK		WALK	**12** Sat.
9 Wed.	WALK		Memo.	

SHANNON LEE It can be argued that he started working towards his 'Definite Chief Aim' with great success in 1970, which is when he did his first film in Hong Kong. All told, I'd say he did a pretty good job in the few years he had.

BRUCE LEE I feel best when I am showing my skill off to the audience. Why? Because, baby, I have worked my X off to be able to do just that, and that means dedication, constant hard work, constant learning and discovering, plus lots of sacrifices.
– *Untitled essay, 1973*

LINDA LEE CADWELL When he first got the offer to go over to Hong Kong his injury was healing well and he said, 'Well this is it. This is my opportunity. This is something I have to do.' So then he started training even more to be ready for that.

I have clearly written down
a description of my DEFINITE
CHIEF AIM in life, and I will
never stop trying until I
shall have developed sufficient
self-confidence for its attainment

1971 一九七一年

1972 一九七二年

香港

HONG KONG

BRUCE LEE
IN MY OWN PROCESS
LETTER EIGHT

I hope my fellow martial artists would open up and
be transparently real, and I wish them well in their own
process of finding their cause.

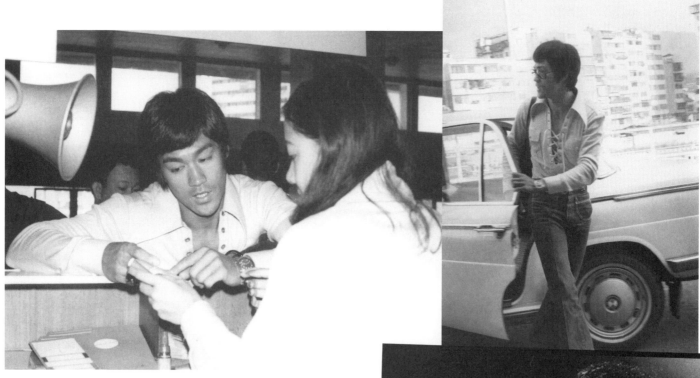

SHANNON LEE He had to create his own projects because the projects he wanted didn't exist. And ultimately he had to leave Hollywood to then come back again.

BRUCE LEE Depending on one's level of understanding, the movie industry nowadays is basically a coexistence of practical business sense and creative talent, each being the cause and the effect of the other.

   To the administrators up in their administrative offices, an actor is a commodity, a product, a matter of money, money, money. 'Whether or not it sells' is their chief concern. The important thing is the box-office appeal. In a way they are wrong, yet in a way they are right. I will go into that later. Although cinema is in fact a marriage of practical business and creative talent, to regard an actor – a human being – as a product is somewhat emotionally aggravating to me.

– Handwritten notes, untitled

MOZEZ Some of the experiences he went through in Hollywood and Hong Kong helped him to be the sort of human he is. You can't become like that until you have been through something. You can't have that power until you have the experience of suffering.

Kai Tak Airport, Hong Kong. Bruce returned to Hong Kong in 1971 to pursue his film career and showcase the work he was capable of

Walk On!

DIANA LEE INOSANTO People have no clue how difficult it was back then in the 1960s and 1970s. But he had spiritual grit, to keep forging ahead to realise his vision of his potential. It was culturally and economically difficult.

There was no legal recourse to deal with the inappropriateness of people's comments on Hollywood sets. He had to endure it. And yet, he still had a vision for himself. If he was going to be rejected here in the United States, he was going to make his own opportunities. For him to go to Hong Kong took perseverance and a lot of belief in himself.

In making my own movie *The Sensei*, I thought about him all the time. As a woman of mixed-race heritage, I was tired of casting directors saying I wasn't the right type and agents rejecting me. My mother reminded me about Uncle Bruce making his own opportunities and thank God I had him as a role model. What a role model he was for so many people. Not just for Asian people but people of all races, backgrounds and abilities. He is an example of perseverance. He would always tell my dad, as a metaphor for life, to 'walk on'.

W. KAMAU BELL As a black person growing up in America, you see any number of situations where you can't go down the path that white people go and expect it to turn out well. You have to be willing to adapt, and then you learn about Bruce who is another person who learned to adapt to what was going on.

RANDALL PARK So much of Bruce Lee's journey resonates with me – the struggles he went through both personally and professionally, and his relentless drive despite all those setbacks. When things weren't working for him, he made it happen on his own terms, and that is so inspiring to me. I also see him as someone who blazed so many trails and broke so many stereotypes – something that I hope to do in my own small way throughout my career. To me, the best way to address stereotypes is by being human.

Bruce on the set of *The Big Boss*, Thailand, 1971

THE BIG BOSS

DIRECTORS Lo Wei, Wu Chia-Hsiang
WRITER Lo Wei
PRODUCER Raymond Chow

BRUCE LEE as Cheng Chao-an
MARIA YI as Chow Mei
JAMES TIEN as Hsu Chien

RELEASE DATE 23 October 1971 (Hong Kong)

BRUCE LEE in **THE BIG BOSS** x

NORA MIAO My involvement with *The Big Boss* was brief and I only appeared in one scene with Bruce. But I must say, even in that short time I saw his professionalism and work ethic. He was serious about creating an environment that would make for a good film. Bruce was very aware of what an audience liked and appreciated, and you can see that in his performance by his mannerisms, physicality and charisma. It was a joyful time and a great introduction to working with Bruce.

Bruce and Nora Miao in a promotional photo for *The Big Boss*. *The Big Boss* was the first of two films Bruce did with Golden Harvest – a production company set up by Raymond Chow and Leonard Ho.

Keep your mind on the things you want and off those you don't

SHANNON LEE One of his sayings was 'Keep your mind on the things you want and off the things you don't.' The 'be water' principle is all about hitting an obstacle and then figuring out how to flow around or through it. You have to go to Hong Kong to get the kind of movie roles you want? Then you go to Hong Kong and do that. The important thing to remember is that my father obviously exercised his body, but he also exercised his mind just as rigorously. He was highly self-educated; he read thousands of books. He carried around affirmations and read them every day; he practised the art of positive thinking and constructive doing. These were part of his daily regimen. When you look in the writings, there's not one 'I'm so pissed that this is happening' kind of sentiment. That's not to say that he never got mad; he certainly did. But he did not spend his constructive time on anger. He spent it problem solving and looking forward.

Cast and crew on the set of *The Big Boss*, Thailand, 1971

BRUCE LEE Bruce Lee is a changing person because he is and always will be learning, discovering and expanding. Like his martial art, his learnings are never fixed. They keep changing. At best, Bruce Lee presents a possible direction, but nothing more.

Some significant traits of Bruce Lee which the author finds admirable are his honesty to himself, quality over quantity (to put it in his words, 'I can walk away from millions because it's not right, but I'll be damned if I'll back up an inch from a dime because it has to be so'). Last but not least, he is a hardworking man, although over 90 percent of the superstars who would be in his shoes would be neglecting his worth and would abuse his power.

– In My Own Process, Letter Six

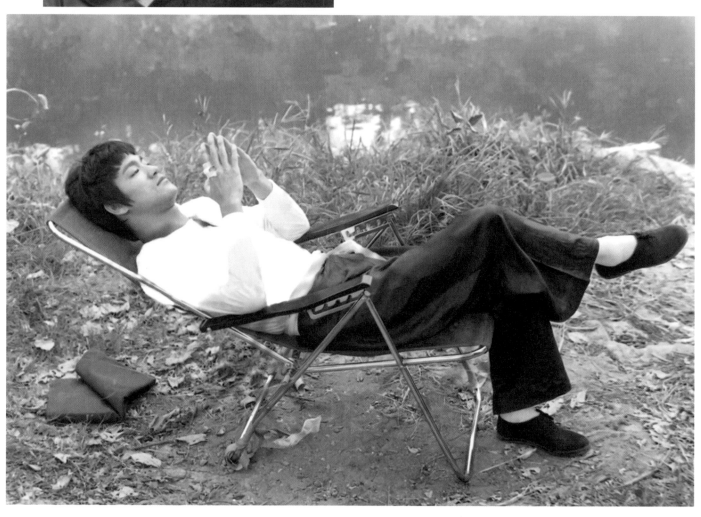

LINDA LEE CADWELL What is great about the movies that Bruce did was that they were an entryway for people to get to know him and then to go beyond that and see what it was about this guy. What did he have? What can he teach me? First people would learn that Bruce was a real martial artist. There were no scenes in his films that relied on camera tricks. Then people would learn that he had a very deep philosophy within him.

Above: Bruce at Golden Harvest, Hong Kong
Left: Bruce on the set of *The Big Boss*, Thailand, 1971

The Chairman
and
The Members of the Exccutive Committee
of
The Friends of Scouting Organization
request the honour of the presence of

Mr. & Mrs. Bruce Lee

at the Gala Premiere of the film
" THE BIG BOSS "
Under the Distinguished Patronage of
H.E. Lt. General Sir Richard Ward, K.C.B., D.S.O., M.C.,
The Commander British Forces
at the Ocean Theatre, Canton Road, Kowloon
On Wednesday, 3rd November, 1971 at 9:30 p.m.

R.S.V.P.
THE ASST EXECUTIVE COMMISSIONER,
THE FRIENDS OF SCOUTING
MORSE HOUSE
COX'S ROAD, KOWLOON
TEL K-673096

COCKTAILS
9:15 P.M.

DONATIONS WILL BE GRATEFULLY ACKNOWLEDGED

BRUCE LEE An actor, a good actor, not the cliché type, is in reality a 'competent deliverer' – one who is not just ready but artistically harmonises this invisible duality of business and art into a successful, appropriate unity. Mediocre actors, or cliché actors, are plentiful, but to settle down to train a 'competent' actor mentally and physically is definitely not an easy task. Just as no two human beings are alike, so too with actors.
– *Notes, untitled*

RANDALL PARK In my opinion, a good actor is always honest, vulnerable and in service of the character and the story.

Above: Bruce and Linda's invitation to the
Big Boss premiere
Right: Action shot from *The Big Boss*

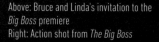

童軍知友社
THE FRIENDS OF SCOUTING
HORSE HOUSE, 9, COX'S ROAD, KOWLOON. TEL. K-673096

Mr. & Mrs. Bruce Lee,

Present.

Confusion at the Jurong Drive-in

29 NOV 1971

Police had to be called in to clear a massive traffic jam caused by about 300 cars at the Jurong Drive-in on Saturday night.

The crowd was there to see midnight show, The Big Boss, a Hong Kong box office hit.

The confusion began when the first few cars at the drive-in were refused entry because they did not have the tickets for the show. But they could not turn around because of the long line of cars behind.

Meanwhile, the entrance was completely choked as more and more cars arrived. Some patrons with tickets for the show tried to get in by the exit entrance.

As confusion reigned, police were called in to help ease the situation. The midnight show started about 45 minutes late.

The Big Boss stars Hollywood actor Bruce Lee.

● Tomorrow—an exclusive interview with Bruce Lee.

nov 29, 1971

The Big Boss premiere, Hong Kong, 1971
Top left: Bruce with actor Han Ying-Chieh and producer Raymond Chow
Above left: Bruce and Linda
Above right: Bruce, Linda, Shannon and Brandon

Premiere of The Big Boss at the Ocean Theatre

NORA MIAO It wasn't until I saw *The Big Boss* premiere in Hong Kong that I and everyone there knew he was going to be a superstar. What he was doing was so new and fresh with a confidence that no one else had. We all knew he was special and would achieve great things in his work.

MOZEZ Most of my work resonates with Bruce Lee's teaching as I like to think there's only one path and one true stream of thought. I like to believe we are all in this stream but most of us become exercised by the vagaries of life and so drift from what we are meant to be.

BRUCE LEE When I returned from Thailand after the completion of *The Big Boss*, many people asked me what it was that made me give up my career in the States and return to Hong Kong to shoot Chinese films. To the above question I find no easy explanation except that I am Chinese and I have to fulfil my duty as a Chinese person.

– *Newspaper article titled 'Me and Jeet Kune Do', 1972*

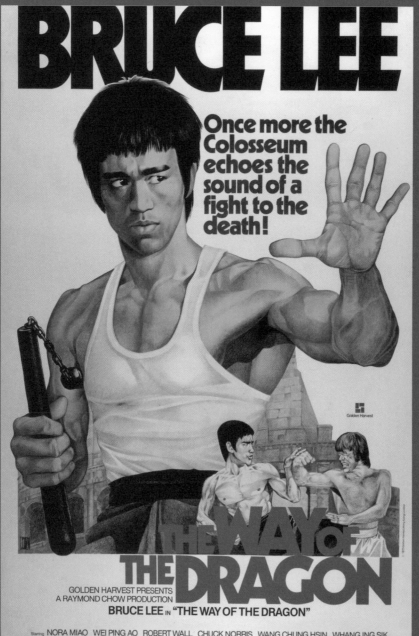

DIRECTOR Bruce Lee
WRITER Bruce Lee
PRODUCERS Raymond Chow, Bruce Lee

BRUCE LEE as Tang Lung
NORA MIAO as Chen Ching Hua
WEI PING-OU as Ho
ROBERT WALL as Bob/Tom/Fred
CHUCK NORRIS as Colt

RELEASE DATE 30 December 1972
(Hong Kong)

BRYANSTON PICTURES Presents
"RETURN OF THE DRAGON"
LITHO. IN U.S.A.
COPYRIGHT (C) 1974 BRYANSTON DISTRIBUTORS INC.
74/2 36

BRUCE LEE
in "THE WAY OF THE DRAGON"

Top: US premiere of *The Way of the Dragon*, Vogue Theater, Hollywood, 1974. The film was retitled *Return of the Dragon* in the US as it was released there after *Enter the Dragon* had made its impact in 1973

Bruce

ENTER THE DRAGON (synopsis)

A young Chinese peasant, Tang Lung, arrives in Rome from Hong Kong, to help a lady friend of his family, Chen Ching-Hua. She has been threatened by local gangsters who want to takeover her restaurant. Both Chen and her employees are deceived by Tang's simple dress and manners. They think he is just a country bumpkin, who is more of a hinderance than an aid to them.

Soon after Tang's arrival, the gangsters appear at the restaurant. They harass and drive the customers away. Their Chinese interpreter demands that Chen signover the deed to the restaurant. Tang who has been in another room misses all of this and as the gangsters are leaving he bumps into one of them and politely apologizes. This further infuriates Chen and the waiters, whose opinion of Tang now hits an all time low.

That evening the gangsters again return to the restaurant for a reply, while the waiters are practising Karate. The gangsters laugh at the theatrical style of fighting. Angered, Tang challenges them and defeats them in and excellent show of his fighting skills. Chen and her employees both are very surprised and impressed with Tang's ability. He is definitely just what they need. But uncle Wang, the restaurant cook admonishes them against the use of force and violence.

The mastermind of the gang orders Tang's assasination. When this fails, they gang up on him and force him to leave Rome. Tang refuses and physically throws the gang out of the restaurant. Undaunted, once again the assasin tries to kill Tang. While Tang is chasing the gun-man, Chen is kidnapped by the gang and taken to their headquarters where they intimidate to sign over the deed. Tang gathers the waiters and together they storm the gang's stronghold and rescue Chen.

The gang leader hires an international Karate champion from the United States in an all out attempt to kill Tang. Tang meets the American in the Roman Coliseum and like gladiators they fight to the death. Having finished off the American, Tang learns that Uncle Wang has been secretly working for the gang all along. As Tang is confronting him with this, uncle Wang is fatally wounded by the bullet meant for Tang. Tang is saved by the speedy arrival of the police. His mission accomplished, he returns to Hongkong for his next assignment.

- END -

Synopsis for *The Way of the Dragon* (the 'Enter the Dragon' working title was dropped and then picked up again for the later film of that name)

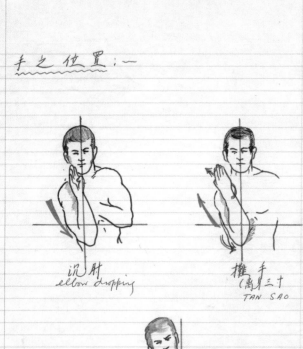

手之位置：—

沉肘
elbow dropping

攤手
(漏身三十
TAN SAO

Park Sao
slapping Hand

—外拍手走外門—

少林派三十六要穴節錄：—

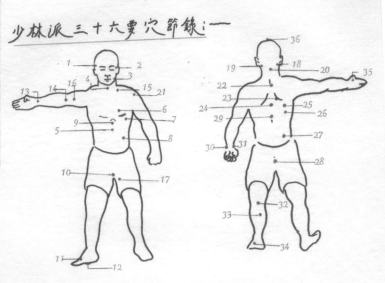

NORA MIAO Bruce wrote, produced, directed, acted and did everything else in between for *Way of the Dragon*. That film was his baby, an expression to the world of what he could really do.

As a director, Bruce seemed to know what everyone needed to bring out their best. I think because he was used to both the Western and Eastern ways of thinking, he was able to find common ground with all the actors and produce something that to this day remains one of the most exciting martial arts action films.

The Way of the Dragon, **1972**
Top left and above: Fighting notes and drawings
Top right and left: Bruce on set

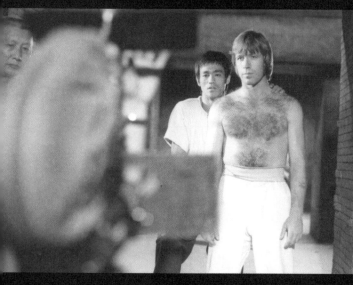

KUNG FU-KARATE

Cast

Tang Lung .... BRUCE LEE
Chen Ching Hua .... NORA MIAO
Kuda .... CHUCK NORRIS
Robert .... BOB WALL

Executive Producer .... BRUCE LEE
                                      RAYMOND CHOW
Director .... BRUCE LEE
Screenplay .... BRUCE LEE
Written by .... BRUCE LEE
Martial Arts Choreography .... BRUCE LEE
Assistant Director .... CHIH-YAO CHA'NG
Film Editor .... CHANG YAO CHANG

TOP PHOTO: BRUCE LEE AND NORA MIAO; BOTTOM PHOTO:
CHUCK NORRIS (L) AND BOB WALL (R) POSE FOR THE
CAMERA BETWEEN SETS.

The Way of the Dragon, **1972**
Top: Bruce and Chuck Norris on set
Middle left: Bruce with Jon Benn, Paul Wei,
Nora Miao and crew on set
Middle right: Bruce with Bob Wall and
Chuck Norris

On location in Rome with Raymond Chow (top
and middle right) and Nora Miao (above left)

The Fight At The Coliseum

(Warm-up).

(1). C.U. of Chuck.

(2). C.U. of Bruce.

Or better yet, be angle →
↑ Over head shot with Cat in foreground. a shot

(3). ~~tracking shot~~ of Chuck as he moves toward Bruce and stops.

(4). M.S. of Bruce.

(5). M.S. of Chuck as he unties his belt and takes off his jacket.

as he also "begins" to take
(6). M.S. of Bruce ~~taking~~ off his jacket.

Slightly lower shot over the shoulder.
(7). ↑ M.S. of Chuck as he smiles bends his wrist turns and shakes his head, Bruce just about takes off his

BRUCE LEE The word 'superstar' really turns me off because the word 'star' is an illusion. It's something that the public calls you. You should look upon yourself as an actor. I'd be pleased if someone said, 'Hey man, you are a super actor!' That would be much better than superstar.

– *The Pierre Berton Show, September 1971*

DIANA LEE INOSANTO My father said that if you look at the fight scene in *Way of the Dragon*, symbolically it is about Bruce Lee's character examining the situation and creating in real time Jeet Kune Do itself. Learning to adjust, to adapt to Chuck Norris's character's movements.

NORA MIAO I thought the storyline fitted well with the history of ancient Rome and the gladiators. Bruce did a great job getting that across.

The Way of the Dragon, **1972**
This page and opposite: Bruce and Chuck Norris
on set
Opposite: Choreography notes for the
Colosseum fight scene with Chuck Norris

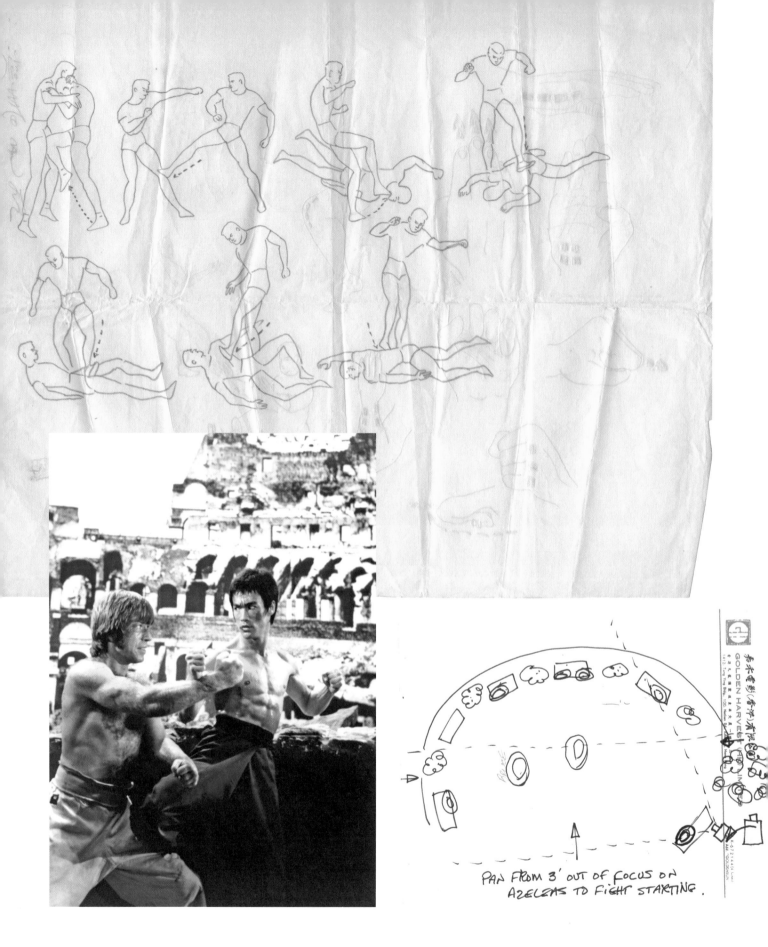

PAN FROM 3' OUT OF FOCUS ON
AZELEAS TO FIGHT STARTING.

The Way of the Dragon, 1972
Right: Bruce and Chuck Norris in the Colosseum
fight scene

W. KAMAU BELL It's funny – the thing Bruce Lee is known for is his fighting, yet his movies will tell you that fighting is a last resort. If you look at *The Big Boss* he is really trying not to get involved until he has no other choice. In *Fist of Fury* he feels so disrespected by the Japanese and they continue to disrespect him in his school until the only thing he can do is whoop their butts. Then in *Way of the Dragon* he's brought in to solve a problem. Fighting is always a last resort, even if you're the best at it. Then there's also the idea that just because you win the fight it doesn't mean you're happy or that your life is better. At the end of *Enter the Dragon* he is exhausted. There's not this hero victory laugh that you see in a lot of American movies. You might be a hero, but it doesn't mean you'll be happy.

notes on Way of Dragon

Above: Bruce, Chuck Norris and crew on set
Top: Bruce recording voice-overs

The Way of the Dragon, 1972
Top left: Personalised leather script-holder
Top right: Bruce making notes on the script
Above: Bruce during filming

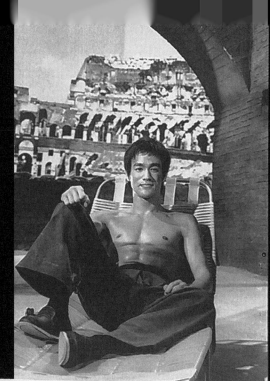

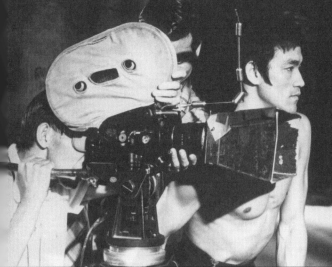

SHANNON LEE My father was an artist of life so it's hard to say where that path would have ultimately led him. He definitely would have continued to be a creative and make his own projects. He directed, produced and starred in *Way of the Dragon*, his third film, so I know he would have gone on to do more of that. At the same time, I can only imagine that a person that thought and explored as he did would have continued to carve a unique path through life. It's hard to say what it would have looked like because he was evolving all the time and part of what he believed was that it was his

page ③

COLISEUM FIGHT

PART 1 (continue)

(1). A low angle [see previous shot] shot, Chuck also turns and faces Bruce — get a good fist angle.

(2). C.U. of "Bruce" "head-on" as he advances

(3). head-on C.U. of Chuck as he also advance

(4). over head shot of two combatant walking to firing line

(5). C.U. of Bruce as he tunes in and "really" stare

(6). C.U. of cat staring.

(7). over the shoulder M.S. of Chuck as he also stare then slowly bows and gets into position.

(8). zoom close-up over the shoulder shot of Bruce's slight acknowledgement, we pull back Bruce get into a stance.

(9). C.U. of cat's screams

(10). C.U. of Bruce's sudden scream and move out of shot two knee shot favouring Bruce as he

a) groin kick
b) hook kick
c) jumping hook kick → chuck retreats

JOE LEWIS For a guy that only weighed 138 pounds, he hit extremely hard. He could hit as hard as a heavyweight. He had [powerful] fast-twitch muscle fibres. It was something he was born with. He trained hard, he worked on a lot of his stabiliser muscles and his speed. I always thought he was the fastest guy that ever stood in front of me. He had incredible Zen level focus and you didn't know when he was going to squeeze that trigger. He always knew when you weren't ready. He had blinding speed, especially with his hands, and I know this because he stood in front of me and popped me a few times. I always told people I know how hard Bruce Lee could hit, I know how fast he was, because he nailed me. I know what real Jeet Kune Do is because I got popped with it a few times.

The Way of the Dragon, **1972**
Above: Bruce on set
Right: Scene notes, under the working title 'Enter the Dragon'

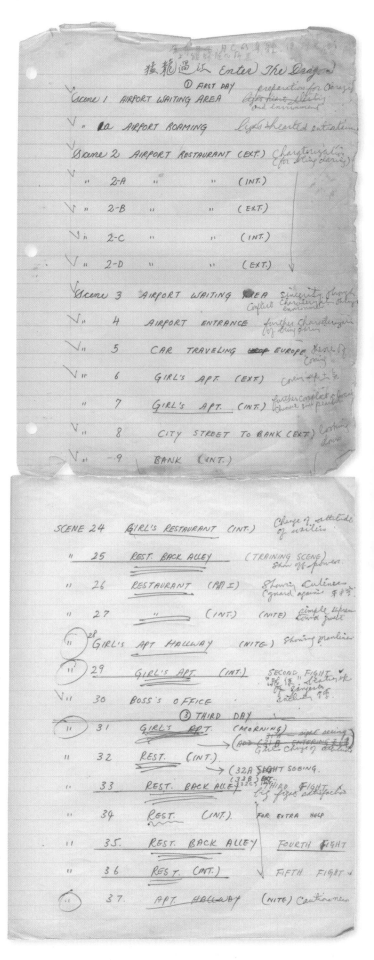

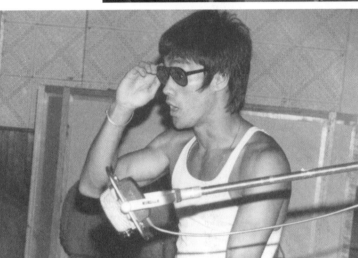

JON BENN Bruce joked all the time on the set of *Way of the Dragon*. He was always showing off because he was the best and he knew it. One time, I was smoking my cigar, waiting for the next scene and Bruce knocked the ash off my cigar with a kick but the cigar didn't move at all. He was that accurate.

RANDALL PARK I don't remember when I first became aware of Bruce Lee – I feel like I was always aware of him. I was born shortly after he passed away, and by that point it seemed that he was already a legend. His movies were always playing on the television, and some of my earliest childhood memories revolved around my brother and me watching them and then play-fighting afterwards – wanting to be as cool as he was. Like most boys of my age, we'd make nunchucks out of rolled up newspapers and some twine, and we'd try to copy his moves. He has been an inspiration throughout my life.

Bruce on set with Jon Benn

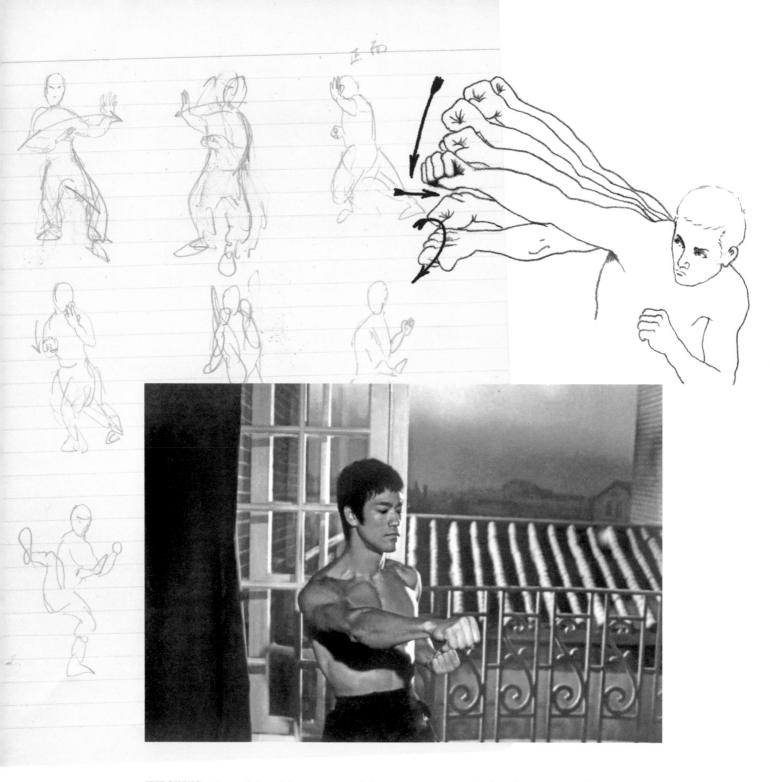

JEFF CHANG A lot of the debates around Bruce question whether he was a real martial artist. Could he have beaten Muhammad Ali? Would he beat Conor McGregor now? But it completely misses the point and is in line with this fascination that our culture has with violence.

The Way of the Dragon, 1972
Top: Fighting technique sketch
Above and opposite: Bruce on set

TED WONG *Way of the Dragon* very much represented the kind of real fighting that Bruce would do off camera.

W. KAMAU BELL I think black people connected with Bruce Lee and martial arts in general because it was a way to defend ourselves without the use of guns. There was a sense of vulnerability, of not being protected in the world, of having to do for yourself and be careful. Even though we're all under the Second Amendment, they didn't want us to have guns; as the Black Panthers learned there's no Second Amendment if you're black. So the Black Panthers trained in self-defence, as did the Nation of Islam and a lot of the people around Martin Luther King, Jr. It was a way for us to feel again, to sharpen our minds and bodies so that we weren't helpless.

TED WONG The way he moved, the way he executed the technique – he was so crystal quick. People try to imitate him and they are very good but somehow they don't have his charisma.

MOZEZ There was something about Bruce that was more than a movie star and it showed in his work. You could feel his energy through the screen. Consequently, I became interested in what made the man who he was. It became evident reading through his writings that there was much more to him.

LINDA LEE CADWELL A lot of people say that Bruce's charisma comes across in his films. They can connect with him. It's him that makes the movie.

DIRECTOR Lo Wei
WRITERS Lo Wei, Ni Kuang
PRODUCER Raymond Chow
CHOREOGRAPHER Bruce Lee

BRUCE LEE as Chen Zhen
NORA MIAO as Yuan Li'er
RIKI HASHIMOTO as Hiroshi Suzuki
ROBERT BAKER as Petrov
WEI PING-OU as Wu En

RELEASE DATE 22 March 1972
(Hong Kong)

Chinese Connection
(Fist of Fury)
"Repaying evil with justice"

LITTLE DRAGON
ANG LEE

When I was 17, I went with my whole family to the Nandu Theatre in Tainan to watch *Fist of Fury*. It was the biggest theatre in our town, built out of a beautiful old baroque building. I knew at the time that *The Big Boss* was a record-breaking hit in Hong Kong but it had been censored in Taiwan due to violence, so *Fist of Fury* was my first experience watching Bruce Lee on screen. It was like nothing I had ever encountered before. I had seen martial arts movies, but never at that level of shocking exhilaration. The dojo fight especially had a jaw-dropping impact on me and the rest of the theatre. It hit a nerve that was both thrilling and empowering at the same time. The emotion, the rawness, the rhythm, timing, body language and visceral screams all spoke to me on a primal level. It made me feel alive.

There is something about the way that Bruce Lee performs on screen that touches an audience's subconscious. It's a very private kind of individual self-expression that calls out to the collective in a way that is honest and truthful, while at the same time entertaining and effective. It was clear to me that Bruce's films were not like any other action movie, with flurries of dazzling stunt sequences and dynamic shots that are exciting to look at but lack significant emotional content. The archetype of the triumphant underdog is a universal one, not unique to Bruce's work, and overcoming adversity is at the very heart of the cinematic language. Those types of stories have roused our spirits and inspired us for thousands of years. What then is so different, so captivating about Bruce Lee? His self-expression tells a story through movement; the way that he breaks down an opponent on screen is visceral, motivated, and saturated with meaning. It reveals to us the unique perspective of a man who was a dynamic balance of contradictions and dualities.

Many aspects of Bruce defy simple definitions. He was a child of two continents and a foreigner in both worlds, yearning for belonging. He had one foot in Eastern philosophy and culture and the other in Western rationality and logic, and he brought the two together in a bilateral exchange that enriched both traditions. That duality made him interesting, and his search for belonging led him in the direction of movies, to the creation of fantasy and imagination. On one hand, we have a man who developed one of the most sublimely efficient hand-to-hand fighting methods that the world had ever seen through his ability to strip away deceptive mental narrative and analyse the bare essence of a thing. On the other hand, Bruce was also a storyteller who was able to generate enchanting fantasy through image and illusion, and who forever changed the way that martial arts are depicted and performed on screen. I am fascinated by Bruce's aspect as an actor, because I think that his inclination towards acting was very important to him, and his determination to be a great performer despite the fact that acting as a career was frowned upon at the time of his upbringing highlights for me the dynamic of individual self-expression in the context of a repressive culture. It emphasises discipline, balance and quiet resilience; to 'be water' and go with the flow rather than assert oneself as a unique human being.

China has been a troubled place for generations, often victimised by internal strife and colonial expansion from the East and West alike. My family has always been on the losing side of history. My parents fled the Communist revolution in China to settle in Taiwan. When I came to the United States I was a minority, but when I return to China, I'm Taiwanese, an outsider. I'm no different from many people in that way, and the years of conflict and confusion of identity gave rise to a kind of collective inferiority complex which is crystallised in the 'sick man of Asia' epithet that Bruce rages against in *Fist of Fury*. Bruce turned that ingrained, defeated stereotype on its head and presented a new picture on screen, an icon of rejuvenating strength for those who felt disenfranchised. He was the Little Dragon that woke an even greater dragon, being 200 years of unvoiced Chinese collective oppression. With his union of East and West he is everywhere an outsider, yet somehow that very duality is what allows him to become a hero to both worlds simultaneously. He draws you in with his martial strength and prowess, fascinates you with his aggression and superlative masculinity, and then you go deeper and learn about his philosophy, his depth as a thinker and a scientist, and that really hooks you. It's a very mysterious kind of power that he wields. His rebellion started with the Chinese people and rippled out to all the smaller communities around the world who felt repressed and marginalised, speaking a message of hope to millions. What is even more compelling is that Bruce worked hard for everything that he attained; nothing was handed to him. He earned every ounce of the muscle, skill and panache that he uses to best his opponents. He transcended our expectations of what it means to be a human being and became something even greater.

I suspect that the compulsion to break the rules, subvert stereotypes and forge a new identity arises in someone who does not feel like they truly belong anywhere. For Bruce, everything that he does is firmly rooted in who he is as an individual. As a person, a martial artist, a philosopher, a filmmaker, or whatever it is that you want to call him, Bruce was a man who through sheer force of will and inexhaustible energy became a legend, and then an icon. Bruce Lee was one of the greatest entertainers who ever lived, because he was able to touch us not just physically or mentally, but in spirit. He was a prophet of both martial arts and action cinema; a cosmic figure who burst into existence like a comet, streaking across the heavens of humanity. His brilliance left us much too soon, but the remarkable impact that he made on the world still inspires us to this day.

ALL MEDIA SCREENING NOTICE

PAGODA FILMS
11 East Broadway, New York, N.Y. 10038 U.S.A. Tel. (212) 964-1825-6

October 10, 1972

FILM: FIST OF FURY   Mandarin dialogue with English & Chinese
sub-titles. Running time: 103 minutes.

TIME: 10:30am, Tuesday, October 17, 1972

PLACE: Pagoda Theater, 11 East Broadway NYC (Chinatown)
north of Chatham Square(Bowery & Mott St)
Ind 'F' Train to East Broadway
Ind 'D' Train to Grand Street
BMT & IRT to Canal Street

*   *   *

FIST OF FURY stars BRUCE LEE the new idol and sex symbol
of millions of Asian female fans and he promises to surpass this popu-
larity in the United States. An expert in Chinese Boxing he may be re-
membered by American audiences for his featured part in the TV series
The Green Hornet.

FIST OF FURY is a blockbuster film in the Southeast Asian
markets grossing $4.8 million in its Hong Kong run. The population of
Hong Kong is 4.8 million. Movie admission is $1.

FIST OF FURY is typical of the Chinese sword movies and
Peking Operas where the Chinese virtues are glorified. The film is set
in 1908 and depicts the drama and conflict between a Chinese Boxing Club
and a Japanese Boxing Club with tragic results. This film has been acclaimed for some of the finest performances of the art of Chinese Boxing.

As a testimony to this super-star on the rise,Warner Bros
is releasing his next film BLOOD & STEEL (English dialogue with American
stars) now in Hong Kong production.

FIST OF FURY will have its American Premiere engagement
at the Pagoda Theater on Tuesday , November 7, 1972

For further information p

W. KAMAU BELL In his movies there was a clear pushback against the man, pushback against state power, pushback against racism. In *The Chinese Connection / Fist of Fury* there's a scene where he can't go into a place because there's no Chinese or dogs allowed. As black kids watching, we understood what that was like. We had felt that kind of state power.

Fist of Fury, 1972
Above: Press release
Right: Bruce on set with Tien Feng and
Nora Miao

NORA MIAO My character in the film, Yuan Li'er, was one of the supporting leads to Bruce Lee's character, Chen Zen. Our characters were to be married and I played a student at the famous Jingwu martial arts school. I think one of the reasons *Fist of Fury* did so well was because we were able to show the strength of both characters and we were equals in many ways.

Though *Fist of Fury* is an action-packed film, I also view it as a love story. There's the love between a man and a woman in a relationship, love for your Sifu (father figure), love for tradition and love for justice and the truth.

DIANA LEE INOSANTO Uncle Bruce was a real advocate for women. He wanted women to be empowered. One of the arts he practised was wing chun; a martial art created by a woman.

NORA MIAO What appealed to me about martial arts films is that a woman could be an equal with a man and even champion over him in a fight. I loved being able to portray a strong woman on screen, especially for the next generation.

Bruce and Nora Miao

KAREEM ABDUL-JABBAR Bruce was a social justice champion. He made inroads against the bigotry in the movie industry and the bigotry against people of colour. It was something that we talked about often, about how they had Asian people depicted in a certain derogatory way, black people in a certain derogatory way and he was against that. He wanted people to see Asians as real, not as Charlie Chan or Hey Boy, which were such narrow depictions of Asians. I had studied Chinese history and I knew that the British wouldn't let the Chinese or dogs into parks in Hong Kong, which Bruce wasn't aware of. I told him about it and it ended up being a scene in *Fist of Fury*. It was also about the depiction of the female martial artists. People don't understand Bruce's feminist underpinnings – the women he taught were ready to compete. He was way out there in terms of his philosophy in relation to the martial arts.

Fist of Fury, 1972
Bruce in fight scenes

LINDA LEE CADWELL He used to call his way of martial arts 'scientific street fighting' and that's what he wanted to portray. In the past martial arts movies had a lot of fairy tale scenes of men flying through the air, that sort of thing. There is a place for that but that's not what he wanted to do.

NORA MIAO Bruce stressed realism within his action choreography. He didn't like the trends of the martial arts films in Asia – he felt that they were over the top with ridiculous stunt tactics and uncoordinated movements. Bruce's films had a life and energy that were new and exciting, that raised the standard in what was being done in Hong Kong at that time. He changed action cinema.

The whole process was a great learning experience for me, watching how Bruce handled, created and lifted up the martial arts action genre to a new level. Before, it was a business with the same old routines as far as fighting and choreography. The experience of watching Bruce Lee create a fight scene was like watching numerous movies within one.

W. KAMAU BELL He didn't have guns, he didn't have knives, he was doing it with the force of his body. With Martin Luther King, Jr. it was the march on Washington, not the attack on Washington, not the palace coup on Washington. It was just a walk and people thought, what's that going to do? With Bruce, it's not about him going to get a bigger gun to take care of the thing, it's about 'I've trained myself to do this and so I'm gonna do this.'

ROBERT LEE All his life when he was watching films he would see Chinese stereotypes. He said, 'If I ever have a chance to go on film or on stage I will never portray something like that. It's a disgrace to Chinese culture.' He wanted to bring the image of Chinese culture up to the same level as other cultures. I'm glad that he did that.

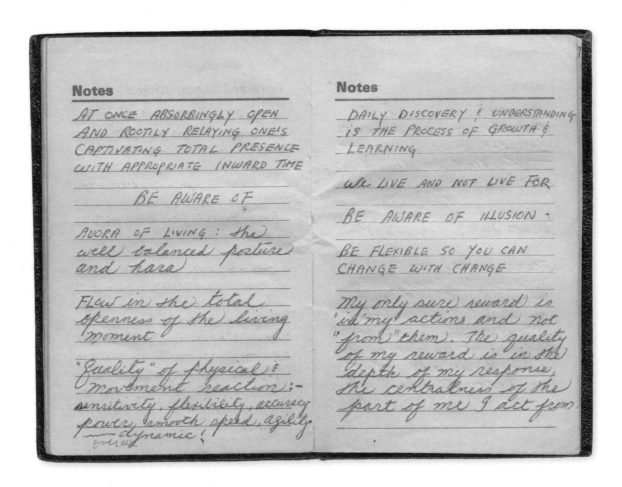

SHANNON LEE He himself encountered a lot of racism. He was not 100 percent Chinese and when that was discovered he was forced to study away from the other students in his wing chun class as a teen. He grew up, first in Japanese-occupied Hong Kong and then in British-ruled Hong Kong. Though the majority of the population was Chinese, the Chinese were treated like the minority in many ways. All of this instilled in him a sense of having to do for himself and a desire to approach the world in a 'human first' way.

Affirmations in 1972 pocket diary

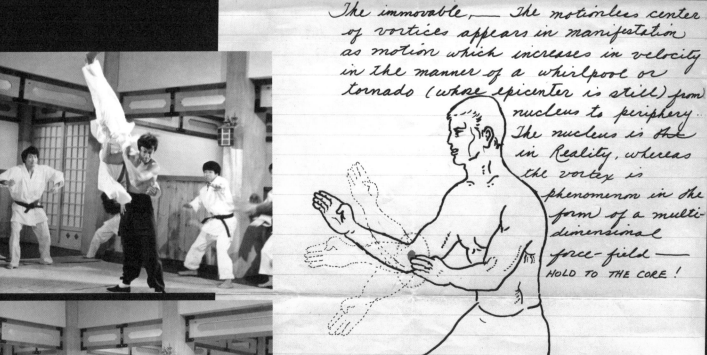

The immovable,— The motionless center of vortices appears in manifestation as motion which increases in velocity in the manner of a whirlpool or tornado (whose epicenter is still) from nucleus to periphery. The nucleus is the in Reality, whereas the vortex is phenomenon in the form of a multi-dimensional force-field — HOLD TO THE CORE !

ROBERT LEE What he did on screen was something that nobody had done before. He just played a true, sincere martial artist and he really managed to project that.

Fist of Fury, 1972
Top left: Fight scenes
Top right: Fighting notes and illustration
Above: Bruce with Linda, Shannon and Brandon on set

W. KAMAU BELL The older I get the more I like *Fist of Fury* because it deals with the same kind of work I do in challenging racism. It's about a guy standing up to racism from the Japanese who are oppressing the Chinese people. As a kid I don't think I understood that, but the older I got, the more I understood and researched the history behind the film. Also, the fight in it is meaningful because it's about reclaiming dignity. There's a scene where the Japanese people come to the memorial service of Bruce Lee's character's teacher and they show up with this giant framed Chinese calligraphy that says 'sick man of Asia'. Bruce Lee's character later takes it back to their school, kicks everybody's butt and says, 'We are not the sick men of Asia!' Apparently when it played in Chinese theatres people were cheering at that scene. For me, as a black kid, even though it wasn't about me, I could see how it related to the struggle of black people in America.

Fist of Fury, 1972
Scene in which the Japanese present a sign
that reads 'sick men of Asia'

SHANNON LEE My father wanted to bring an authentic representation of an Asian man to the screen in the West. That was definitely his goal. And so he worked really hard to be excellent so that when the opportunities came he was ready. And all he had to do was show up in his full skill and presence to create that representation.

BRUCE LEE In every big thing or achievement there [are] always obstacles, big or small, and the reaction one shows to such obstacles is what counts, not the obstacle itself. There is no such thing as defeat until you admit one to yourself, but not until then!
– *Letter to Grandmaster Jhoon Rhee*

SHANNON LEE The one thing my mom always said was that he just took people at face value. He didn't look at what ethnicity they were or whether they had money or didn't have money. He just wanted to know if you were sincere.

DOUG PALMER Bruce Lee was a genius, in the sense that he could look at things – especially martial arts systems – from a different perspective than others and utilise them in unique ways. He was also a revolutionary. He revolutionised the martial arts world, and the way martial arts were portrayed in film. He overturned our stereotype of the Asian man and brought an appreciation of the martial arts to a mainstream audience. His approach to the martial arts, and to life, influenced many people in other disciplines as well.

Left: Promotional photos for *Four Seas Weekly* magazine, Ocean Terminal, Hong Kong, 1972
Above: *Fist of Fury* screening, Hong Kong

Notes

A goal is implied but the need seems to be for direction — — to feel in the process of becoming.

When I listened to my mistakes I have grown.

There will never be means to ends, only means. And I am means. I am what I started with, and when it is all over I will be all that is left. Of me.

Top left: Affirmations in pocket notebook
Above: Bruce's reading glasses. Although they were broken, Bruce kept them as a reminder of the difficult times he had faced in the past. Later, in 1972, he purchased a pair of Persol sunglasses (pictured top right and opposite)

SUCCESS BEGINS WITH A FELLOW'S WILL —

STEVE AOKI He was fighting for this role in *Kung Fu* and it was given to David Carradine and that's just how the industry was. They gave an Asian role to a white guy and it was seen as totally OK, even though Bruce Lee had the reputation and the prestige. It's crazy to know that that even happened when he was killing the game.

W. KAMAU BELL The thing that connects black people to Bruce Lee is his fight against racism. *Warrior* was an idea that he pitched around Hollywood, but he was turned away because they couldn't let an Asian man be the star of a TV show. So what did they do? They stole the idea and created the show *Kung Fu* starring David Carradine, and Bruce is not honoured as the creator of the show.

Bruce posing with his red Mercedes outside
Golden Harvest, Hong Kong, and a selection
of his platform shoes

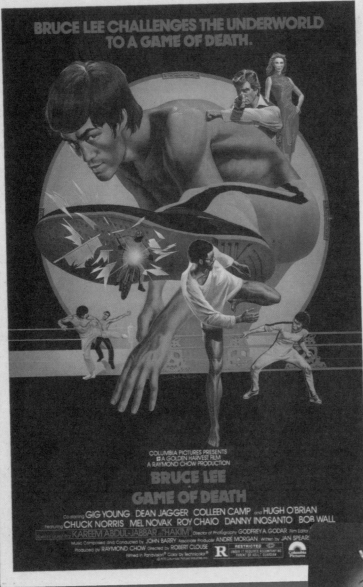

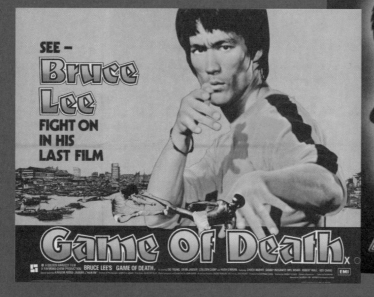

DIRECTOR Bruce Lee
WRITER Bruce Lee
PRODUCERS Raymond Chow, Bruce Lee

BRUCE LEE as Hai Tien
KAREEM ABDUL-JABBAR as Mantis
JAMES TIEN as Mr Tien
CHIEH YUAN as Yuan
DAN INOSANTO as Dan
JI HAN-JAE as Chi
LEE KWAN as Mr Kuan

RELEASE DATE 23 March 1978 (Hong Kong)

死亡的遊戲

The Game of Death

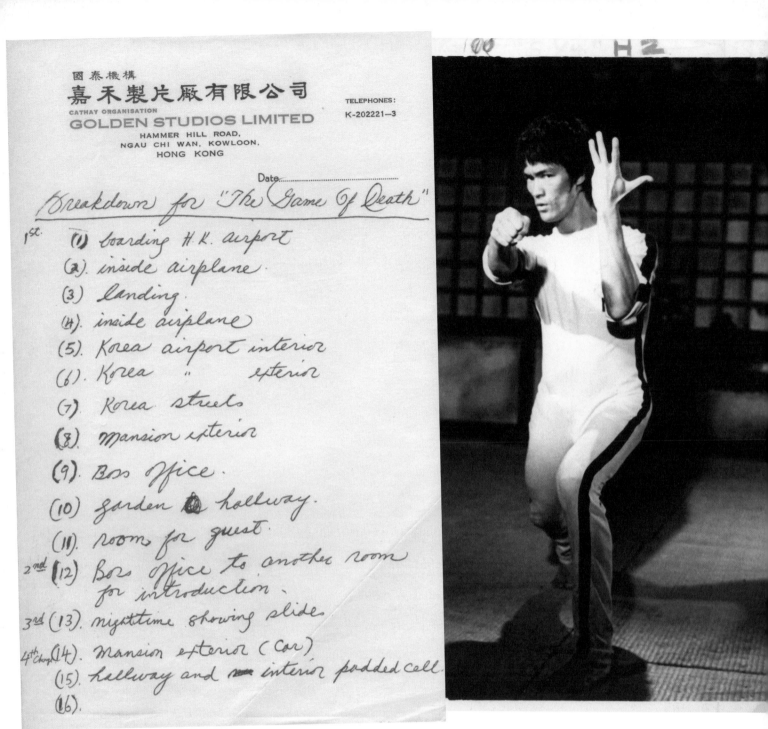

國泰機構
嘉禾製片廠有限公司
CATHAY ORGANISATION
GOLDEN STUDIOS LIMITED
HAMMER HILL ROAD,
NGAU CHI WAN, KOWLOON,
HONG KONG

TELEPHONES:
K-202221—3

Date

Breakdown for "The Game Of Death"

1st.
(1). boarding H.K. airport
(2). inside airplane.
(3). landing.
(4). inside airplane
(5). Korea airport interior
(6). Korea " exterior
(7). Korea streets
(8). mansion exterior
(9). Boss office.
(10). garden & hallway.
(11). room for guest.
2nd (12). Boss office to another room for introduction.
3rd (13). nighttime showing slides
4th Chap (14). mansion exterior (Car)
(15). hallway and interior padded cell.
(16).

KAREEM ABDUL-JABBAR We had planned that we could be in a film together and I would be the villain and we pulled it off. There I was, a basketball player acting in a martial arts movie. Awesome.

STEVE AOKI *Game of Death* was an incredible film. It's like a video game where he was fighting all these different characters. There's a fight with Kareem Abdul-Jabbar which is just so epic – him in his yellow jumpsuit and Kareem looking like he's 90 feet tall. It always pops in my head, he's just a badass.

Game of Death, 1972
Above left: Breakdown of scenes
Above right and opposite: Bruce and Kareem
Abdul-Jabbar on set

PICTURE (B)
ATTACKING PLAN (進攻計劃)

Game of Death, 1972
Above and opposite: Scene drawings and
research photographs, South Korea

DAN INOSANTO The pagoda in the film had so many levels. I think the bottom level was guarded by karate people, the second level was guarded by a praying mantis gung fu group and I was on the third level. The top level was the 'temple of the unknown', where Bruce faced Kareem Abdul-Jabbar.

Game of Death, 1972
Top: Bruce and Dan Inosanto
Above: Fight scenes with James Tien

他 body, and the limits of his body, are used to work towards his own defeat.

"THE BIGGER THEY ARE, THE HARDER THEY FALL"

拳尚循勢使敵勁不外也外也變宜怎臨則如用乱良

BRUCE LEE Bear this in mind once you go into action and grapple with an opponent. Strive to keep him off-balance, regardless of his size. So keep moving faster than he and pay absolutely no attention to his size, fierce facial contortions, or his vicious language. Your object is always to attack your opponent at his weakest points, which are mainly gravitational, throwing him off balance, and applying leverage principles so that his body and the limbs of his body are used to work towards his own defeat.'The bigger they are, the harder they fall.'

– Essay titled 'Psychology in Defense and Attack', circa 1961

Game of Death, 1972
Top left: Bruce writing notes while visiting Shaw Brothers studios
Top right: Fighting notes in a pocket notebook
Above: Rehearsing fight scenes with James Tien

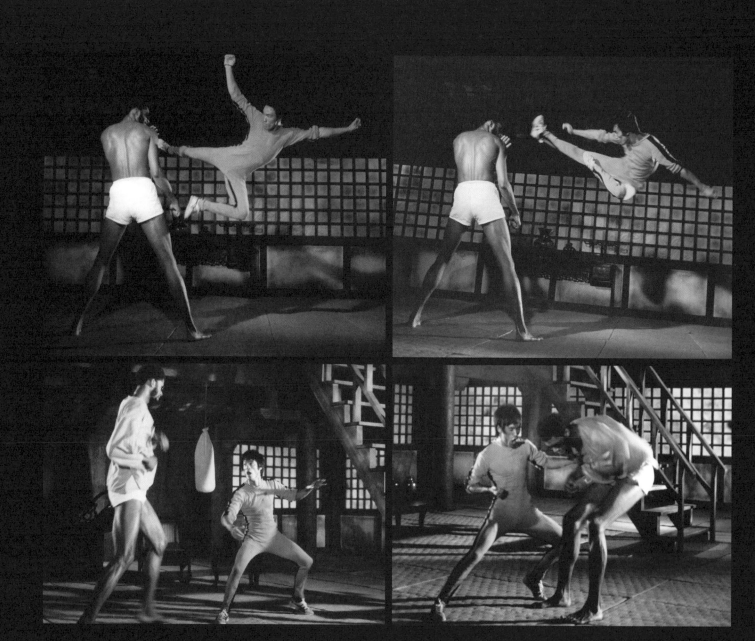

KAREEM ABDUL-JABBAR On the outside, it seemed like an unlikely friendship: between a 5 foot 8 inch Chinese American martial artist and a 7 foot 2 inch African American basketball player. But we were both more than that. We shared an interest in music, the arts, philosophy and improving the lives of the people that looked like us. I am often asked what the average person can do to make the world better? And I say, 'Make a friend that doesn't look like you.' I know that doesn't solve our deep embedded problems of systemic racism, but motivating people to recognise that there is a problem starts with creating empathy with others. Bruce was funny, charming, disciplined, dedicated and sometimes goofy. I learned from him that real change is only possible when marginalised groups join together to fight for everyone's rights, not just their own. He singlehandedly made martial arts an international phenomenon and in doing so made millions of friends that didn't look like him. All of our lives have been made better because of Bruce.

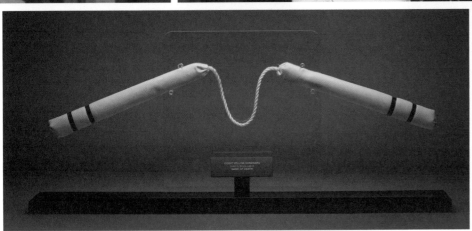

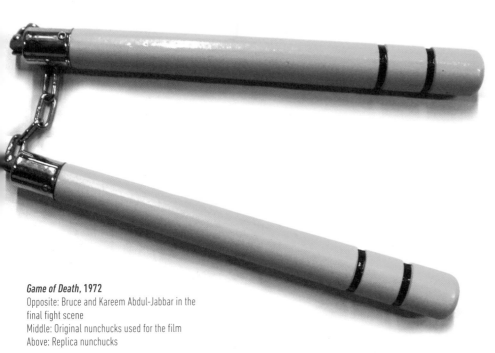

Game of Death, 1972
Opposite: Bruce and Kareem Abdul-Jabbar in the
final fight scene
Middle: Original nunchucks used for the film
Above: Replica nunchucks

DOUG PALMER Bruce's mastery of the martial arts techniques in his repertoire was obvious, but what impressed me even more was the fact that he was constantly evolving. In his family's words, when Bruce left Hong Kong for the States at the age of 18 he was a 'good to above average' martial artist, but when he returned four years later he manifested a 'very special talent that is rarely found on this earth'. I especially witnessed his evolution during the time I was away at college. Every time I came home on vacation he had something radically new to show, grafted onto his existing skills as an organic extension.

One time it was his broken-rhythm technique. To demonstrate, he asked me to block a punch. At full speed there was no way I could block his punch, but this one he executed at half speed. His punch seemed to float out and I moved my hand for an easy block. But then the motion of his fist shimmered as if an old-time movie film had snagged briefly before the reel resumed its revolution on the projector; the fist passed my hand right after the block and stopped an inch from my nose. Even after several tries I couldn't block the half-speed punch.

BRUCE LEE Ordinarily, two people (of more or less equal ability) can follow each other's movements. They work in rhythm with each other. If the rhythm has been well established, the tendency is to continue in the sequence of the movement. In other words, we are 'motor set' to continue a sequence. The person who can break this rhythm can now score an attack with only moderate exertion.

– Lee Family Archive

Game of Death, 1972
Above and opposite: Bruce and Kareem Abdul-Jabbar in the final fight scene
Opposite top left: Notes on grappling and joint-lock techniques

) grappling and joint lock arch combinations

. spread Eagle groin
lot.

TWO HITS, SIDE ARM THROW
AND ELBOW.

HIT.

1

2

HIT

block hit

Squeeze.

3

4

5

6

elbow, hand
rake, right
thrust if necessary

7

The handshake twist.

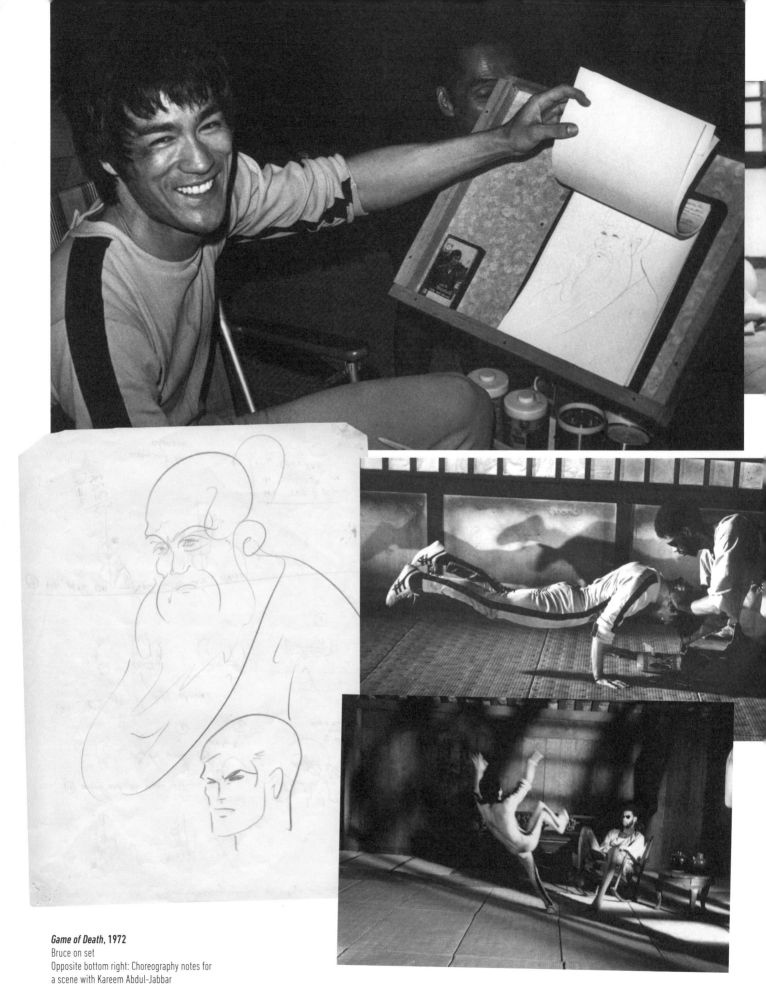

***Game of Death*, 1972**
Bruce on set
Opposite bottom right: Choreography notes for
a scene with Kareem Abdul-Jabbar

(1). M.S.
As Bruce jumps up 田 is thrown across the screen.
Bruce looks / cut.

(2). a shot of 田. He is dead.

(3). M.S of Bruce as he advance, he looks and stops. Camera
zooms into a C.U.

(4). 拳 Bruce 門. a shot of Kareem.

(5). C.U. of Bruce after flash dialogue as we pull back
a Neutral shot of the men standing he gets into
a stance.

(6). Kareem steps backward and sits down, as we
track in to his a C.U.

(7). C.U. of Bruce as he yells. cut

(8). As Bruce launches a kick Kareem out
reaches him with a drops full punch, knocking
him down.

(9). 拳足 Bruce falling and he looks.

(10). Kareem rocking, stops and rises

(11). Two men shot
Bruce rises and as he attempts something
Kareem. slghs lead stop, rigos hook kick.
(Both faces blocks Kareem, rigos lead and knocks Bru
launches) down with a hook kick. Bruce rises and drops as

IN MY OWN PROCESS 我的自我探索過程

1973

一九七三年

**BRUCE LEE
IN MY OWN PROCESS**
LETTER EIGHT

I have always been a martial artist by choice, and actor by profession. But, above all, I am hoping to actualise myself to be an artist of life along the way.

FILM
EXCHANGE

NOLASCO FILM
EXCHANGE INC.
greets
"ROBEN
THEATRE"
*on its
inauguration*

李小龍兼主導演

Soon In 3 Theaters
• THE WILD NEW WORLD
    in Technicolor
plus: Cartoon Shows
• FIST OF UNICORN
directed and starring
BRUCE LEE
• FABLES TALE OF HANS CHRISTIAN
ANDERSEN
• THE NEW ADVENTURE OF THE
THIEF OF BAGHDAD
• THE TALE OF KING SALTAN
• MYSTERIOUS ISLAND
• AND SATAN SMILED
• MATALO
• SHERIFF WAS A LADY
• A FACE OF HELL

LINDA LEE CADWELL The idea was that if he moved to Hong Kong and made his films there, he could come back to the States and show them what he could do, which is exactly what he did.

SHANNON LEE *Fist of Unicorn* was one of the projects that Unicorn Chan was trying to get off the ground. He and my father were friends so my father helped Unicorn out because by that time he had gained recognition for his work in Hong Kong.

Fist of Unicorn, **1973**
Shortly before starting work on *Enter the Dragon*, Bruce joined his friend Unicorn Chan on the set of his film to help boost its publicity
Above and opposite: Bruce and Unicorn Chan

BRUCE LEE The undeniable fact is I am becoming a public figure. From a capable Chinese boxer – I'm no strategist, and if you call me vain, I try not to complain (you have your right) – suddenly I am a known actor. Mind you, actor, not star – I've gone through that too. The sad fact is that there are too many people here wanting to be stars rather than quality actors or actresses.

– *Essay, untitled, 1973*

STEVE AOKI It's harder to speak out against racism when you don't have a community that can support you, so having Bruce Lee and these strong role models that kicked everyone's ass, who were trying to save the situation and be who everyone was rooting for, was incredible.

BRUCE LEE Unfortunately, a lot of pictures are done just for the sake of violence without a reason why.

– *The Pierre Berton Show, September 1971*

W. KAMAU BELL TV stations in the 1980s had Black Belt Saturdays or Samurai Sundays and they would show kung fu movies. They would often be called Bruce Lee movies and I thought I was watching Bruce Lee, thinking 'Wow! Bruce has made 100 movies and he looks different in every one of them!' It wasn't until I went to a video store and saw the real Bruce Lee movies that I realised I was watching the imitators of Bruce Lee from the Bruceploitation genre. I rented *Enter the Dragon* for 24 hours and I must have watched it four or five times. I thought, 'OK, this is so much better than anything I've seen before.' For me, though, the Bruceploitation movies were a great amuse-bouche to the real meal that was Bruce Lee. They could certainly sometimes be poor and feel exploitative, but as an American kid I was just happy to meet the concept of this person named Bruce Lee.

LINDA LEE CADWELL Bruce did not invent martial arts movies. They had been made for decades in China, Hong Kong and Taiwan but this was the first time that Western audiences were exposed to these films.

Bruce on set, *Enter the Dragon*, 1973

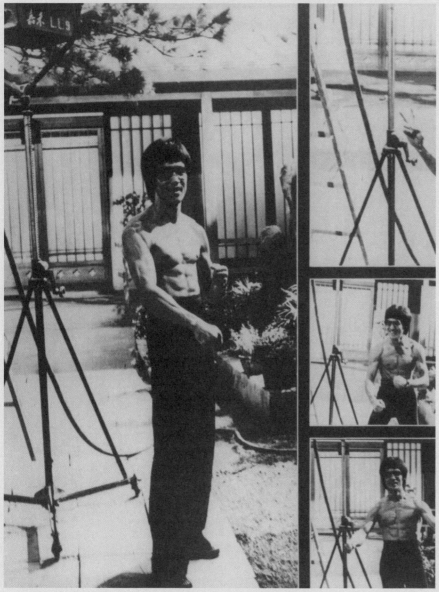

JEFF CHANG Black audiences were some of the first audiences to be exposed to Bruce Lee films for a couple of reasons. Firstly, the Hollywood system was collapsing and a lot of the big studios were dying. There was also a larger event that was happening – white flight. A lot of white people were abandoning the cities for the suburbs and so the movie theatres were abandoned too. This left an opening for new talent, and independent distributors started programming these theatres. These are the folks that make B-movies, the Roger Corman flicks and the avant-garde movies. Often, they were a little shady too and they brought in porn movies and blaxploitation movies, but they also brought in kung fu movies. In the summer, kids could hang out there all day for a couple of bucks and be transported to another time, place and culture.

In the kung fu movies a lot of the values resonated with these kids: brotherhood, loyalty, standing up to the man. It's also about youthful rebellion and kicking ass. Racism and segregation created the context in which these movies were first shown. But the movies also gave these people the tools to think about how to overcome prejudice. How to develop empathy for other cultures, how to see in other people's stories what you see in yourself and how to expand your circle of empathy.

Golden Harvest, Hong Kong, 1973

JEFF CHANG The birth of global popular culture as we now know it really happened in 1973. On 13 April you have the release of Bob Marley and the Wailers' *Catch a Fire*. Just one month later you have three kung fu movies topping the charts as the highest grossing movies in the country. You have *The Big Boss* (released in the US as *Fists of Fury*), then Angela Mao's movie *Lady Whirlwind* (released as *Deep Thrust* to appeal to the porn market) and *King Boxer* (released as *Five Fingers of Death*). On 11 August DJ Kool Herc and Cindy Campbell throw the party that we celebrate now as the birthplace of hip hop. Eight days after that *Enter the Dragon* is released.

Now, you can look at popular culture and see how everything has shifted. Before that, popular culture was dominated by suburban American ideals of whiteness. In 1973, popular culture is all about the urban and what's happening with young people of colour. It's all about the voices of the voiceless. It's where it all began. Without those events taking place we would still be talking about John Wayne.

BRUCE LEE As far as I am concerned (and this is only my personal opinion) an actor is, first of all, like you and me, strictly a human being, and not a glamorous symbol known as a 'star', which, after all, is an abstract word, a title given to you by people.

If you believe and enjoy all those flatteries (yes, we are only human, and we all do to a certain extent) and forget the fact that the same people who once were your 'pals' might just desert you to make friends with another 'winner' the moment you no longer are a winner, well, it's your choice. You own your right (although choice requires some self-inquiry here, it is still your choice; you have that right).

My more than 20 years' experience as an actor has caused me to look at it thusly: an actor is a dedicated being who works very hard – so damn hard that his level of understanding makes him a qualified artist in self-expression, physically, psychologically, as well as spiritually – to captivate.

– *Notes titled 'What Is an Actor?'*

What exactly is an actor?

An actor is, first of all, like you and me, a human being who, in this case happens to an artist. An artist capable of expressing oneself psychologically and physically with realism and appropriateness and, of course, hopefully in good taste. So what it really amount to is the revealation of a person's taste, his educational background, his learning, discovering (sometimes involving much soul-searching in the form of through honest self inquiries) etc etc. Just as no two human beings are born alike, the same hold true for actors.

Film-making is basically a marriage of business administrators or the and art, and in the eyes of the studio and money people an actor is often referred to as a salable product, commodity, box-office holders, etc, etc, difference ———

No matter ti Because you can, as human being, dedicate yourself and train so hard on what you can deliever; well, the money people will listen.

DIRECTOR Robert Clouse
WRITERS Michael Allin, Bruce Lee
PRODUCERS Fred Weintraub, Paul Heller, Raymond Chow

BRUCE LEE as Lee
JOHN SAXON as Roper
JIM KELLY as Williams
AHNA CAPRI as Tania
SHIH KIEN as Han
ROBERT WALL as O'Hara

RELEASE DATE 19 August 1973 (US)

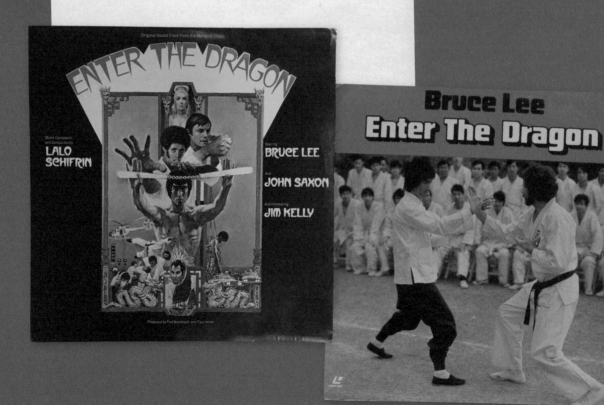

REPORT - ENTER THE DRAGON

    "With a cry the two of them rush together and the fight begins. This is to be the smashingest, fuckingest fight ever put on Eastman Kodak #5254 color stock."

Thus it's impossible to know what might be missing here and whether or not it's indispensable.

****

BRUCE LEE I have discovered another quality over the spread of a decade. I have long been in the process of discovering through earnest personal experiences and dedicated learning that ultimately the greatest help is self-help. That there is no other help but self-help, to honestly do one's best, dedicating oneself wholeheartedly to a given task, which happens to have no end but, rather, is an ongoing process.

– *In My Own Process, Letter Seven*

SHANNON LEE Even though my father never published his process essays himself (they were published decades after his death), the communication of these ideas still existed in his actions, in the way he presented himself in life and in films. But because he documented all of this process as well as lived it, it also exists for us to hold in our hands and know him more intimately.

Enter the Dragon, **1973**
Above left: Bruce on Han's island
Above right: Bruce's character, Lee, talking to the master monk, played by Roy Chow

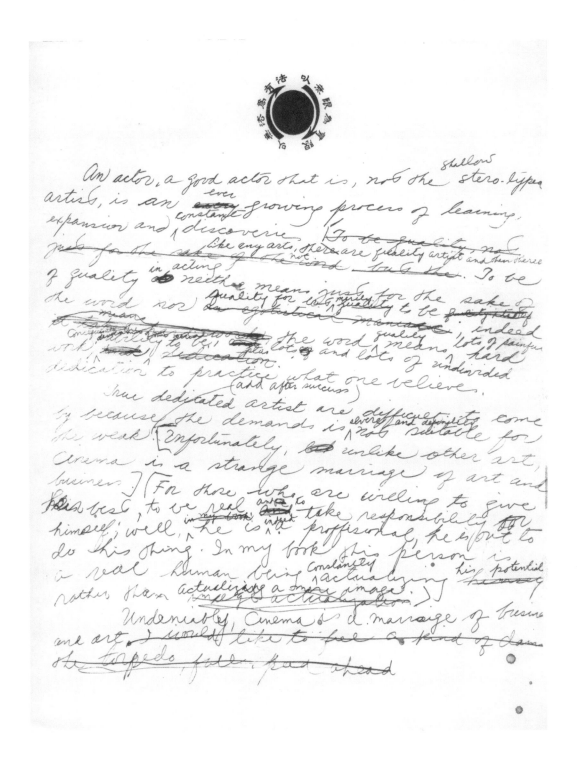

LINDA LEE CADWELL He was very prolific in writing down his feelings and his thoughts and his direction. It's never good to lie to people but it's especially important not to lie to yourself, so he wrote down his feelings, what he wanted to do. He thought he could do better in some areas so he wrote it all down.

It's very interesting to read his drafts and see what he crossed out and replaced. He was always thinking like that and that's also the way he thought about his scripts. He'd keep making changes until he ended up with producing the product that we see today.

Notes on acting

SARLUI
OBUS

李小龍

協和

猛龍過江

Enter The Dragon

SHANNON LEE *Enter the Dragon* was a co-production between Warner Brothers and Concord Productions, which was my father's production company in Hong Kong. It was the first Hong Kong/Hollywood co-production, and it was the opportunity my father had been waiting for. He'd been wanting to make a Hollywood film as a leading man and so he halted production on *Game of Death* in order to pursue this project. He poured his heart into the making of *Enter the Dragon* – rewriting script pages, crafting fight choreography, negotiating with the studio back in Hollywood for all manner of

SHANNON LEE *Enter the Dragon* was the dream opportunity for my father – a Hollywood feature for him to star in. That said, Hollywood billed it as a double lead in case their gamble on my father didn't pay off, and in part due to the intense concern surrounding the xenophobia of audiences at that time. But my father didn't worry himself with this. He knew he had the goods even if others weren't sure. He was ready to make the absolute most of this opportunity to show the Western world the glory of Chinese gung fu and to express himself in a true on-screen representation of a Chinese man.

(to be filmed in Hongkong)

Asia's leading action-actor Bruce Lee will become the first Chinese to star in a Hollywood production early next year.

The film, a joint venture between Warner Brothers and ~~Hong Kong's~~ Concord Film Company, is expected to make Bruce internationally known as the Orient's Clint Eastwood.

The project was decided on this week after Bruce and film boss Raymond Chow had the loose end tied up in a recent trip to the United States.

Earlier, a Warner Brothers representative, Fred Weintraub, had been in Hong Kong for preliminary talks with Concord.

Bruce will be given top billing in the Bond-type thriller called Enter The Dragon, a title Bruce once intended for his directing and scripting debut, The Way of the Dragon.

Also in a starring role
~~In second male lead~~ will be American actor John Saxon, who co-starred with Marlon Brando in Southwest to Sonora.

Acclaimed action film director Robert Strauss will be at the helm.

Shooting will be completed in Hong Kong and the States within a period of about three months.

Cameras are scheduled to start rolling in Hong Kong's Golden Harvest studios on January 8.

The story will centre on Bruce as a Chinese super-agent in a bid to save the world.

Bruce, at the present stage, would not tell more about the film's plot elements.

Nor is he willing to disclose details of the co-operation between Concord, partnering Mr ~~Chow~~ and ~~Bruce~~ himself, and Warner Brothers.

unlike the past
" But I am happy to say that the deal is made on a fair and square basis," he pointed out.

" And I've made sure that the film will not bring any disgrace to my countrymen."
...END...

LINDA LEE CADWELL This was the breakthrough movie, the Hollywood connection. It was his ticket into Hollywood. Bruce wanted to elevate the image of a Chinese person and expose people to Chinese culture, which at over 5,000 years old, has so much to offer the world. It was not well represented in Hollywood at the time. For decades, when there was a Chinese character it was played by a Caucasian actor with makeup on.

Enter the Dragon, 1973
Top left: Press release
Top right: Bruce relaxing on set with cast and crew
Above: John Saxon, Linda and Bruce on set

SHANNON LEE It is so fascinating to me that in the midst of all that was going on my father was writing these multiple drafts of these articles to himself. At the very top of letter one he writes, 'At the moment I'm wondering for whom I'm writing this organised mess. I have to say I'm writing whatever wants to be written. I have come to the realisation that sooner or later what it really amounts to is the bare fact that even an attempt to really write something about oneself demands, first of all, an honesty to oneself [and] to be able to take responsibility to be what we actually are.' It's almost like he is saying to himself, 'I am taking this huge step in my life, and I need to pause and remind myself who I am.'

In these writings are so many quotes about the need to have direct inquiry into oneself and the need to be completely honest. The idea that there is no help but self-help, that all knowledge is self-knowledge, he was working a lot of this out through pen to paper. And then he stepped up and created *Enter the Dragon*, and I think his writings gave him the energy and clarity of vision he needed to do that.

BRUCE LEE This is the first article I am going to write about me, myself. It is not the usual goings on. Yet at this moment I am wondering for whom I'm writing this 'organised mess'. I have to say I am writing whatever wants to be written. Also included in these feelings is an urge to be as honest as I can – oh, I know, I am not being summoned by the court to tell the whole truth and nothing but the truth.

– *In My Own Process, Letter One*

Bruce's character, Lee, talking to the master monk

MOZEZ Even though Hollywood gave him so many problems, he was able to forgive them. They didn't understand what they were doing so he was able to reach that place where he didn't want to fight. You know you have the power to destroy but you don't because you understand.

SHANNON LEE There was only one problem. The script was terrible. So terrible, in fact, that my father was adamant that the writer be fired and sent back to California while he himself feverishly rewrote the majority of the screenplay. Of course, the studio didn't listen to my father and kept the writer in Hong Kong, making small tweaks to what was initially titled 'Blood and Steel' and later the inventive 'Han's Island'. The original script had none of the iconic scenes that exist today.

BRUCE LEE A really trained, good actor is a rarity nowadays – that demands the actor to be real, to be himself. The audiences are not dumb today; an actor is not simply demonstrating what he wants others to believe he is expressing. That is mere imitation or illustration but it is not creating, even though this superficial demonstration can be 'performed' with remarkable expertise.

– *Notes, untitled*

SHANNON LEE It was of utmost importance to my father that this film reflect his art and culture accurately and with depth. This was his moment to show the world who he was and what a Chinese gung fu man could do, and he was not going to settle for mediocre. So he rewrote the script and submitted his rewrites to the producers. He also argued back and forth with the studio over the title. He wrote numerous letters to Warner Brothers petitioning for this name change from 'Blood and Steel' to 'Enter the Dragon'.

Enter the Dragon, **1973**
Background: Note on the back of the script
reading 'The main thing is Lee!'
Top left: Bruce on set

(BLOOD AND STEEL)

ENTER, THE DRAGON

ENTER THE DRAGON
BLOOD AND STEEL

An Epic Of The Martial Arts

one [213] 843-6000

HYATT REGENCY HONG KONG

Sent June 8, 1973

Dear Ted,

Just a note to let you know this "18 years old" has arrived safely.

Do consider carefully in regard to the title of "Enter The Dragon"

(1). This "unique" dragon (the Chinese the spiritual, etc.) is not one of Won Ton Kung Fu flicks from H.,

(2). With the rightful publicity in can tell on the screen as as outside that this dragon has broken the all time record consecut. like you said "is come across.".

I really think this is a good title and like I said do think it over carefully because "Enter The Dragon" sugge the emergence (the entrance) of some one (a personality) that is of quality Time is pressing. Ted. (over)

BLE
001612

67 Nathan Road G.P.O. Box 5648 Kowloon Hong Kong B.C.C. Telephone 3-662321 Cable: Hyatt Hongkong

NNNN
ZCZC HRB5
HXHK CO U
TDVYBURBA

BRUCE LEE
41 CUMBER
TELEPHONE
KOWLOONTO

DEAR BRUCE

AS REQUESTED WE HAVE GIVEN HE TITLE STILL FURTHER THOUGHT
AND HAVE TAKEN GREATLY INTO ACCOUNT YOUR PREFERENCE AS WELL
THE TITLE WILL THEREFORE BE ENTERED THE DRAGON
LOVE TO YOU AND LINDA
TED ASHLEY

COL 41 472-1904

Enter the Dragon, 1973
Top right: Early script with original title
Above: Letter from Bruce to Warner Brothers chairman, Ted Ashley, explaining his request for the film title to be changed
Left: Telegram from Ted Ashley, confirming the name change

W. KAMAU BELL I think if he'd lived we would have seen a lot more of his philosophy in his films. He was clearly a philosophical person and he was starting to have more control over his films as he became a bigger star. *The Big Boss*, for example, isn't filled with philosophy but by the time you get to *Enter the Dragon* you can feel the fact that this is a philosophical pursuit in addition to a physical one.

Enter the Dragon, 1973
Top right: Robert Wall

SHANNON LEE The first day of shooting finally arrived, and the Hong Kong crew and the American crew were there, poised to begin, with various translators on set to help the two crews communicate with each other. My father, however, was a no-show. He refused to come to set. The final script had been issued and it did not incorporate the pages he had written. None of his changes had been made. The crew started filming what shots they could that did not involve my father, and my father stayed in our house and refused to come to set until the changes were made.

The standoff continued for two weeks. Tensions were running high among the cast and crew. The producers began to get pressure from Warner Brothers to get the production back on track, and there was only one way that was going to happen.

The producers finally gave in to my father's demands. They implemented the script changes he had made and agreed to shoot the film he envisioned.

Enter the Dragon became a global phenomenon and cemented my father as an icon of martial arts and culture.

Cast and crew including cameraman Gil
Hubbs (centre)

BRUCE LEE One more ingredient is that an actor has to be real in expressing himself as he would honestly in a given situation. An actor's problem, though, is not to be egotistical and to keep his cool and to learn more through discoveries and much deep soul-searching. Dedication, absolute dedication, is what keeps one ahead.

– *Notes, untitled*

***Enter the Dragon*, 1973**
Left: Drawings by Bruce
Right: Fight scenes

Top: Set design for Lee's bedroom
Above: Scenes set in Lee's bedroom

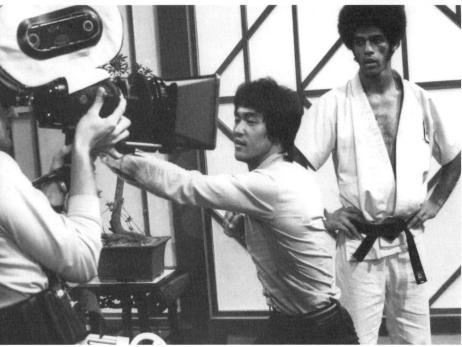

W. KAMAU BELL In black neighbourhoods we weren't just getting Bruce Lee movies. We were getting lots of kung fu movies, some of which we still like – the Wu Tang Clan basically based their whole philosophy around them – but the Bruce Lee movies were the ones we liked the best. For me, and this was pre-internet, I became this Bruce Lee evangelist. Bruce Lee didn't have a star on the Hollywood walk of fame and I read that you could petition for that, so I walked around school with a clipboard, arguing with people about why he deserved a star.

Enter the Dragon, **1973**
Top: Filming the journey to Han's island
Above: Bruce directing a fight scene with Jim Kelly

SHANNON LEE The reason *Enter the Dragon* is good is because Bruce Lee is in it. Otherwise, it's a plot line we've seen a thousand times where you infiltrate the island, you have to fight your way through a bunch of bad guys and you win in the end. But the reason the movie still captivates so viscerally today is because Bruce Lee's contributions and performance are timeless.

Fight scenes with Jackie Chan

SHANNON LEE This guy on the set kept calling my father a Paper Tiger, which meant that he wasn't really a martial artist, he was just faking it. The goading continued until finally my father said, 'Fine, let's go.'

Enter the Dragon, **1973**
Above and opposite: Bruce in fight scenes

CELL BLOCK IN CAVE

RADIO SHACK -

The flying tackle (one guard discovers Lee)

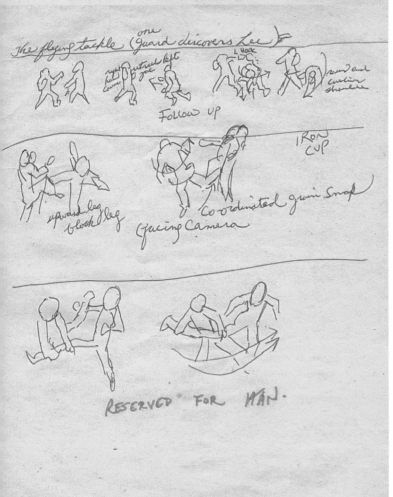

FOLLOW UP

IRON CUP

upward leg block leg

facing Camera

Co-ordinated groin snap

RESERVED FOR HAN.

HAN VS. LEE

DUCK WITH SIMULTANOUS LEFT SWING SPIN
OR DROPPING DOWN
WHILE 手刀 to
mid section

LEE

LEE

DOUBLE Han vs. Lee 1— LEE
R-side L strap/spin Rgt
R-hook - pick up leg
and cross throw

LINDA LEE CADWELL A three-minute fight scene in *Enter the Dragon* might take three days to film, maybe more. Bruce would come home at night knowing he had to go right back and do it again the next day, so everything in our household was centred around fixing his back. His desire was so strong that he was just going to give it his all.

LEE VS. HAN
(SECOND PART)

NOTE:- SEE INSIDE FRONT COVER PAGE

POSSIBLE FACTORS NOT IN CHRONOLOGICAL ORDERS. } DOUBLE FOR SPECT CULAR FALL

(4)(A) LEE 指拳 TAY 勞8 AI: HAN 腿 as lee finishe combination & swings LEFT CLAW-BLADE (REPETE AS WEAPONS) in OBVIOUS FASHION WHICH LEE IMMEDIATELY COUNTERS WITH RIGHT HOOK KICK. HAN BLOCKS WITH right hand.

(B). HAN Right foot advances with right bottom fist downward TOWARD LEE'S LEFT SHOULDER. LEE retreats left foot and counters with and then right stomach uppercuts which slows Han WHILE LEE'S left blocks hand hangs on Han's right bottom fist

(C). LEE she ___ Body tilts toward Han right flank lift Han right hand and as Han attempts to SWIPE IN WITH HIS LEFT WEAPON.

quick twist, left up left hand change to Bow & arrow now ___ waist to explode, change direction of (look profile)

(D). Then turn head on to screen and jumps up to stomp oppon get kick and

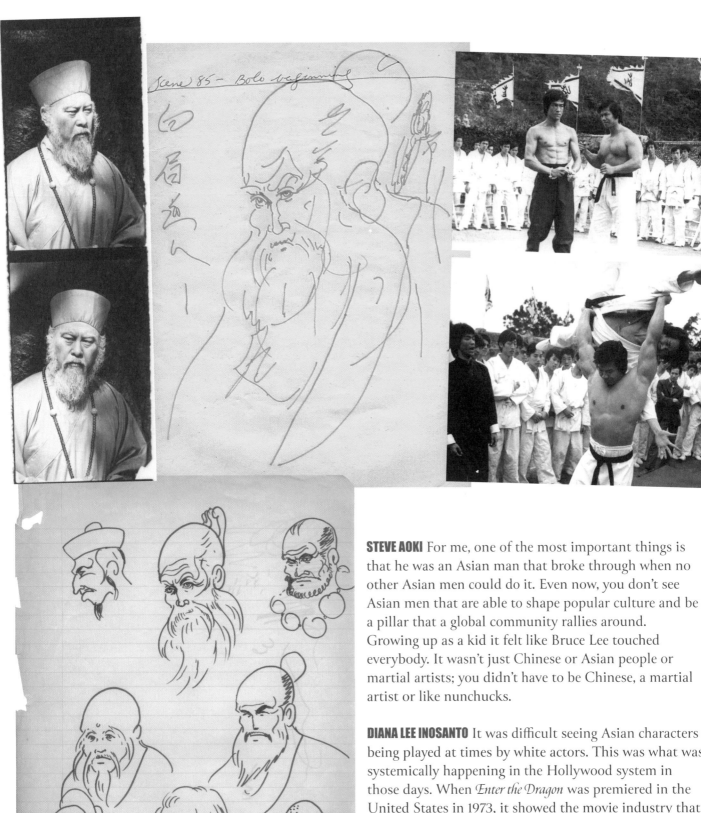

STEVE AOKI For me, one of the most important things is that he was an Asian man that broke through when no other Asian men could do it. Even now, you don't see Asian men that are able to shape popular culture and be a pillar that a global community rallies around. Growing up as a kid it felt like Bruce Lee touched everybody. It wasn't just Chinese or Asian people or martial artists; you didn't have to be Chinese, a martial artist or like nunchucks.

DIANA LEE INOSANTO It was difficult seeing Asian characters being played at times by white actors. This was what was systemically happening in the Hollywood system in those days. When *Enter the Dragon* was premiered in the United States in 1973, it showed the movie industry that an Asian man could take a leading role, which had such an impact.

Enter the Dragon, **1973**
Left: Scene with master monk, played by Roy Chiao
Above: Fight scenes with actor Bolo Yeung

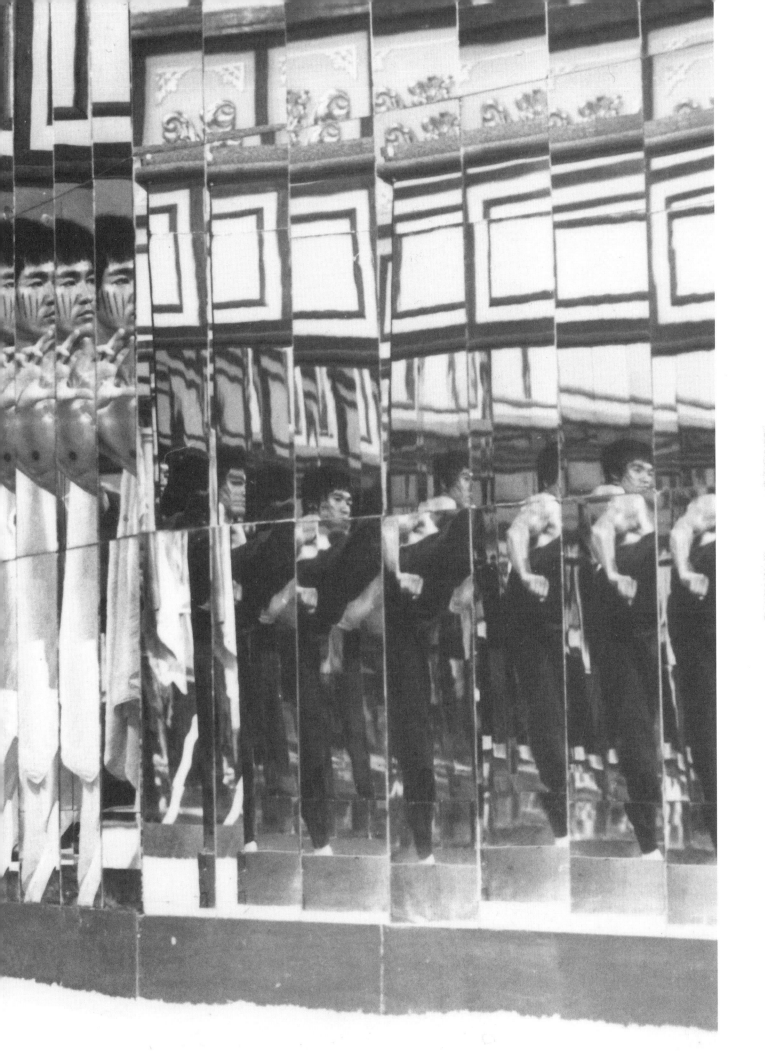

BRUCE LEE When you punch (making sure not to hurt any camera angles) you have to put the whole hip into it and snap it and get all your energy into it and make yourself into a weapon.

– *The Pierre Berton Show, September 1971*

W. KAMAU BELL Bruce Lee is just part and parcel of a worldwide culture and there will always be another generation discovering him in new ways and reinterpreting him. When you see the pro-democracy protesters in Hong Kong holding up signs that say 'be water' you realise that he is always going to be reinterpreted and examined by future generations. I don't think anything will stop that other than the end of the world.

Enter the Dragon, **1973**
Above and opposite: Bruce in fight scenes

KAREEM ABDUL-JABBAR All our favourite movies are about a corrupt official that's trying to come down on some people and the martial arts people protect them. That's the story and Bruce knew how to portray that, and the essence of that excited and inspired people. We'll be thanking him for years to come.

MOZEZ I first became aware of Bruce Lee back in Jamaica when I was a kid. I remember watching *Enter the Dragon* and that was the start of my fixation with anything Bruce Lee, which continued for years. Bruce Lee was a phenomenal figure in Jamaica. I remember in the school playground everyone wanted to be him.

BRANDON LEE My dad left a wonderful legacy and I meet people all over the world who really admire him and his work and they are very positively affected by it too.

JAMES COBURN Bruce Lee was a good friend of mine, we were very close. He was a groovy guy. I was very sorry to see him go. His whole life was related to martial arts. He lived, breathed, fought, moved, dedicated to his highest principle of self-evolution. Bruce Lee was a guy who demanded of himself great excellence. He was a true artist in that sense. He created himself and in that way I think he was an unusual man. He was beautiful. The perfection he achieved was awe-inspiring. The fastest person you've ever seen. I miss him daily.

ANG LEE Accepted as neither fully American nor fully Chinese, Bruce Lee was a bridge between East and West who introduced Chinese gung fu to the world, a scientist of combat and an iconic performing artist who revolutionised both the martial arts and action cinema.

GEORGE TAKEI Bruce Lee was a groundbreaking actor, director and martial artist whose legacy continues to inspire and captivate audiences. His philosophy of self-actualisation and his dedication to his craft have left an indelible mark on the world.

JEFF CHANG All stories of people who die young are stories of lost potential. What happens is that we fill the gap left by the big shadow of that person's passing. Bruce's long shadow has to do with how we might be able to imagine an underdog rising up against oppressive forces. He did it in a way that was mould-breaking because he's a 5-foot-8-inch, 135-pound guy, who is an immigrant, darker skinned and doesn't speak the King's English. What makes Bruce legendary is that he seems so unlikely to become a hero of ours, and in that way he gives every kid hope that they might be able to take control of their destiny.

LINDA LEE CADWELL Bruce saw what was mostly the finished product of *Enter the Dragon*. They were still doing a few edits but he was pleased with what he saw.

JET LI Bruce Lee is a consistent cultural force so it's hard to believe that he passed away so long ago. I only saw his films for the first time in 1974, the year after he died. In the 1970s, I had the chance to travel to many countries around the world and whether it was in Africa, Europe, the Middle East, Asia or the United States I would hear people mention Bruce Lee's name. He was adored universally. Only later did I have the opportunity to watch all his movies and his interviews and that left a deep impression. He not only possessed a transcendent martial arts style, he was also highly educated and a deep thinker. He was a philosopher and a martial artist. In addition, his confidence in Chinese culture influenced generations of people globally.

Every human has a body and is born and will die, but there is a certain type of person whose spirit will always live on. Those people are legends. Bruce Lee is a legend and he will continue to live on in the hearts of many people for generations on end.

Screening of *Enter the Dragon*, Grauman's
Chinese Theatre, Hollywood, 29 August 1973

P.S. Here are the first playdates for "Enter The Dragon":

New York	Loew's State And Orpheum	August 22
Los Angeles	Grauman's Chinese Theatre	August 29
Boston	Savoy	August 22
Philadelphia	Fox	August 29
Baltimore	Hippodrome	August 29

BRUCE LEE These few paragraphs are, at best, a 'finger pointing to the moon'. Please do not take the finger to be the moon or fix your gaze so intently on the finger as to miss all the beautiful sights of heaven. After all, the usefulness of the finger is in pointing away from itself to the light which illumines finger and all.

– Essay titled 'Jeet Kune Do: What It Is Not', circa 1971

SHANNON LEE He didn't just have a handful of great quotes and ideas, he actually lived those ideas. Whether you know he was a philosopher or not, when you're looking at him move on screen, you can sense there's something more to him. It's like you can see his soul in motion.

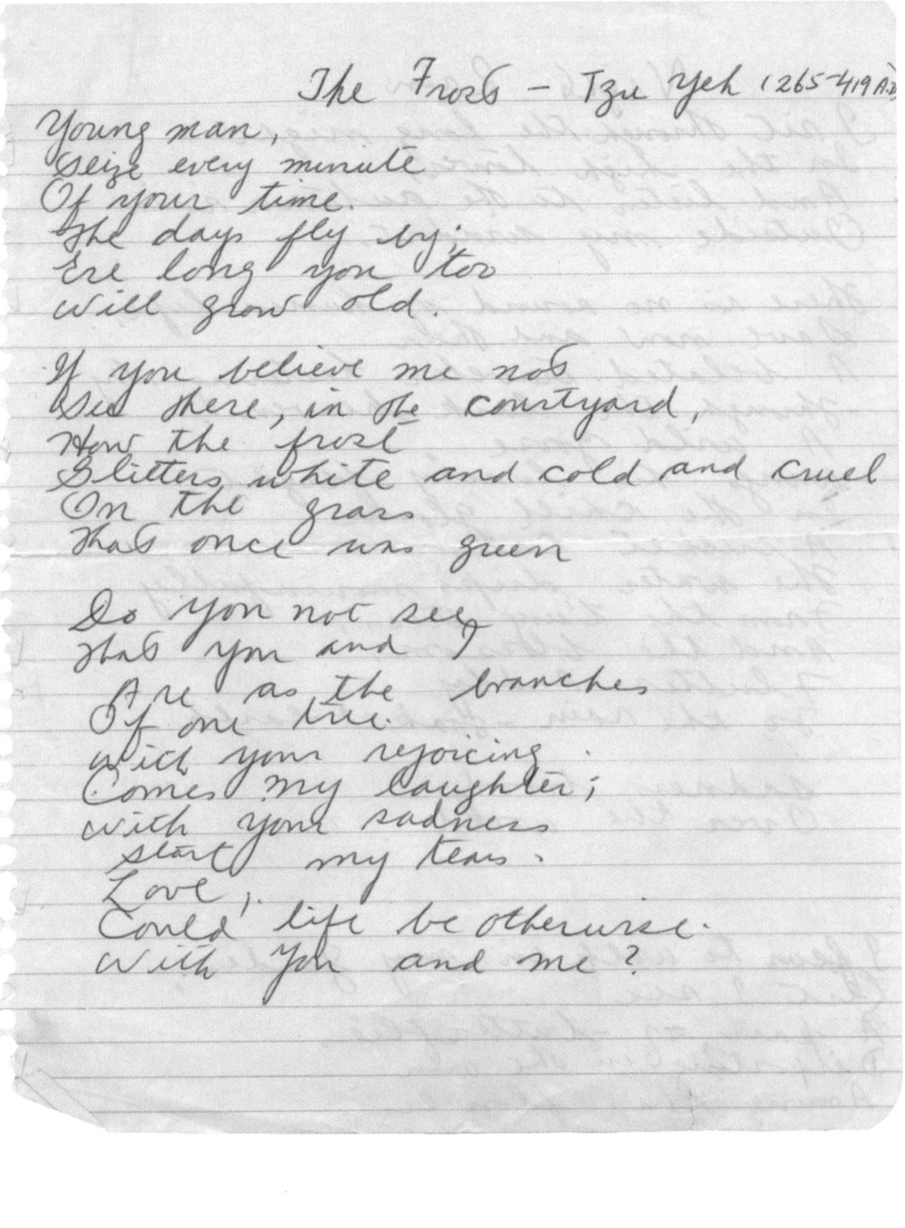

The Frost — Tzu Yeh 265-419 A.D.

Young man,
Seize every minute
Of your time.
The days fly by;
Ere long you too
Will grow old.

If you believe me not
See there, in the courtyard,
How the frost
Glitters white and cold and cruel
On the grass
That once was green

Do you not see
That you and I
Are as the branches
Of one tree.
With your rejoicing;
Comes my laughter;
With your sadness
Start my tears.
Love,
Could life be otherwise.
With You and me?

THE FROST BY TZU YEH
TRANSLATED BY BRUCE LEE

Young man,
Seize every minute
Of your time.

The days fly by;
Ere long you too
Will grow old.

If you believe me not,
See there, in the courtyard,
How the frost
Glitters white and cold and cruel
On the grass that once was green.

Do you not see
That you and I
Are as the branches
Of one tree?

With your rejoicing,
Comes my laughter;
With your sadness
Start my tears.

Love,
Could life be otherwise
With you and me?

Poem by Tzu Yeh, translated by Bruce Lee

KAREEM ABDUL-JABBAR Very few people can say someone
that iconic was their friend. I've always been thankful for
what he taught me about being real and being open.
If you want to be successful you have to take your time to
know what you're doing. That is the essence of it. If you
don't take that time and have the humility to discipline
yourself, you're not going to get anywhere. That's what I
learned from Bruce.

ROBERT LEE There are three aspects to Bruce's success. First, my dad was involved in the Cantonese opera for a long time, at least 40 years. He was one of the top four in China so you could say that Bruce grew up in a show business family. That is one aspect. The other is that he has a dynamic personality and he can really project that personality on the screen or in front of people. The third thing is that he is very sincere in what he is doing and that is really the most important thing. I still use the present tense when I talk about Bruce because I feel his presence all the time with me. He's always with me and I think that goes for everyone who knows him.

TONY HAWK Bruce Lee has inspired many skaters. He exemplified discipline and finding your own path to success while committed to doing something you love.

STEVE AOKI The legend of all legends. The hero. A hero for me since I was a little kid until now. For all the Asians and Asian Americans out there, you paved the way for us to reach out to our dreams and do the unthinkable and I just want to say thank you from the bottom of my heart and thank you to the family for keeping the legend out there and letting people know about Bruce Lee – the man, the myth, the legend.

AFTERWORD SHANNON LEE

I am continually amazed at how absolutely beloved my father continues to be around the world and how inspirational, motivational and timeless his message can be and is for everyone across the world. His philosophies and practices have been very important to me because the energy that is still alive in them have healed me at a soul level. You can feel the power of his practices when you watch his films. It comes out at you; the characters he played and the themes he engaged with, all came through this portal of personal work that he did on himself and then expressed out into the world through the medium of film and television. And because it was captured in writings and moving images, this energy still exists! It's still relevant; it can still excite, intrigue, inspire and influence. If you let it, that initial excitement you felt about Bruce Lee can lead you into a search for self-knowledge. In seeking to understand who Bruce Lee was at a deeper level through his writings and philosophies, you begin to see yourself reflected there. And what started as his process transmutes into your own.

In many of the drafts of the *In My Own Process* essay, my father calls himself a martial artist by choice and an actor by profession, but what he really considers himself is an 'artist of life'. He goes on to say how what would be most meaningful to him is for somebody to see his performances, or simply see him, and say, 'Now there is someone real!' Proudly, I feel like he accomplished this. We gravitate to him because he exuded an enthusiastic energy, an alive energy, an up energy that resonates with us and draws us to him. We see and, more importantly, feel someone real who had the odds stacked against him, who shouldn't have been able to do what he did. He put the sheer power of his will towards cultivating his own energy coupled with his belief in expressing and sharing what he had within. And now, 50 years after his death, we're still talking about him. I would venture a guess that 95 percent of people know the name Bruce Lee. They might not know much about him, but they know his name, and it is the 'why' of that which excites me about continuing his legacy.

My father was once asked by interviewer Pierre Berton, 'Do you think of yourself as Chinese or North American?' And he replied, 'You know how I like to think of myself? As a human being. Because under the sky, under the heavens, there is but one family. It just so happens that people are different.' And the magic is that Bruce Lee cultivated what was 'different' about him and made it into his super power. His personal process revealed the individuality of his soul, the one uniqueness that we all share, and in so doing he became an icon.

When you're old and
cannot see,
Please wear a glass and
remember me!

good-bye!

Bruce

ACKNOWLEDGMENTS

The publishers would like to thank:

Shannon Lee and Linda Lee Cadwell for inviting us
to be part of such an important project

A special thanks to Kareem Abdul-Jabbar and Tony
Hawk for their Forewords

Thank you to Ang Lee and Jackie Chan for their
outstanding extended pieces written for this book

All of the contributors for sharing their thoughts
and memories

Additional thanks to:
Sydnie Wilson, Deborah Morales, Sandy Dusablon,
David Tadman, Jane von Mehren and the team at Aevitas

The Genesis Team, especially Katy Baker

CONTRIBUTORS

KAREEM ABDUL-JABBAR is a world-renowned basketball player (the NBA's all-time second-highest points scorer), as well as being an author and US Cultural Ambassador. Kareem first met Bruce while he was in college at UCLA and after a meeting at Bruce and Linda's house, Bruce soon became his martial arts mentor. Kareem later went on to star in Bruce Lee's film *Game of Death* as Bruce's final opponent, Mantis.

STEVE AOKI is a renowned twice Grammy-nominated music producer and entrepreneur. At a young age, Steve set up his own record label, Dim Mak, the name of which pays homage to Bruce Lee. As a fighting technique, Dim Mak, or 'Death Touch', has its roots in folklore and focuses on attacking pressure points of the body. The same could be said about how Steve's music emotionally connects with its audience.

W. KAMAU BELL is a comedian, director, producer and 'the world's preeminent Bruce Lee scholar, non-Asian division'. His introduction to Bruce Lee was through Bruce Lee imitation films, also known as Bruceploitation movies. It was Kamau's first experience of an authentic Bruce Lee film, *Enter the Dragon*, that showed him the real talent that Bruce had.

JON BENN was a businessman and actor, best known as the cigar-smoking mob boss in *The Way of the Dragon*. He subsequently became friends with Bruce Lee, wrote a book called *Remembering Bruce Lee* and opened a Bruce-themed restaurant in Hong Kong.

JACKIE CHAN is a prolific actor, filmmaker and martial artist, having appeared in more than 150 films. Before graduating to leading roles, he worked as an extra and stunt double in the Bruce Lee films *Fist of Fury* and *Enter the Dragon*.

JEFF CHANG is an author, historian, activist and writer, with a focus on culture, politics, the arts and music. Born and raised in Honolulu, Hawaii, Jeff grew up with Bruce Lee already established as an icon. Jeff has gone on to write and speak extensively on Bruce Lee and his lasting influence, as well as on his identity as an Asian American and a martial artist.

JAMES COBURN was an actor, who featured in more than 70 films, predominately in action roles. Bruce and James were friends, and it was James who recommended that Bruce get into film. In 1969 the pair began work on *The Silent Flute* with screenwriter Stirling Silliphant. However, Bruce died before the film could be made.

JESSE GLOVER was a martial artist. He has gone down in history as Bruce Lee's first student. Following his work with Bruce, Jesse founded his own method, which he called non-classical gung fu.

TONY HAWK is a professional skater, entrepreneur and founder of the Skatepark Project. Considering skateboarding to be an art form, a lifestyle and a sport, Tony finds similarities in Bruce Lee's approach to martial arts. He is inspired by Bruce's philosophy and his determination to overcome limitations.

GRACE HO was the mother of Bruce Lee. Born in Shanghai, she moved to Hong Kong where she met the Chinese opera singer Lee Hoi-chuen. The pair married and had five children: Phoebe, Agnes, Peter, Bruce and Robert.

DAN INOSANTO is a martial arts instructor, head of the Inosanto Academy of Martial Arts and the leading authority on Jeet Kune Do. Dan first met Bruce Lee in 1964 during the International Karate Championships and the pair went on to become training partners. Along with Taky Kimura and Bruce Lee, Dan was one of the instructors running the Jun Fan Gung Fu Institutes set up by Bruce.

TAKY KIMURA was a martial artist and certified instructor of Jun Fan Gung Fu. A close friend to Bruce, Taky was also one of his students and later went on to lead the Jun Fan Gung Fu Institute, along with Bruce and Dan Inosanto.

NANCY KWAN is an actor, who has appeared in films around the world, finding early fame in Hollywood. Nancy met Bruce Lee during the filming of *The Wrecking Crew* where he was on set as the karate advisor.

ANG LEE is a director, producer and writer, whose notable works include *Sense and Sensibility*, *Crouching Tiger, Hidden Dragon*, *Brokeback Mountain* and *Life of Pi*. Ang's first experience of Bruce Lee on screen was watching *Fist of Fury* in his native Taiwan, which had a big impact on him.

BRANDON LEE was an actor, martial artist and son of Bruce Lee. Trained by his father from a young age, he followed Bruce's path into martial arts and acting, beginning his acting career in Hong Kong. In 1993, during the filming of *The Crow*, Brandon was killed on set as a result of an accident involving a jammed prop gun. His death prompted changes in safety standards on film sets, still in place today.

ROBERT LEE is a Hong Kong musician, performer and the younger brother of Bruce Lee. In 1966 he founded the Hong Kong beat band called the Thunderbirds and the group quickly gained fame. He later moved to Los Angeles and stayed with Bruce for a brief period. After his brother's death, Robert released an album dedicated to him called *The Ballad of Bruce Lee*.

SHANNON LEE is a writer, CEO of the Bruce Lee Family Companies, Chair of the Bruce Lee Foundation and the daughter of Bruce Lee. Shannon dedicates her time to promoting her father's legacy, philosophy and life through education and entertainment.

LINDA LEE CADWELL is a retired teacher, writer and the widow of Bruce Lee. Linda met Bruce as a student of his gung fu classes. The pair married in 1964 and had two children, Brandon and Shannon.

DIANA LEE INOSANTO is a martial artist, actor, director, author and goddaughter of Bruce Lee. As the daughter of Dan Inosanto, Diana grew up with Bruce Lee as an important figure in her life and Bruce's philosophy continues to influence her today.

TEXT CREDITS

JOE LEWIS was a martial artist, professional kickboxer and actor. Joe trained privately with Bruce, who was keen to demonstrate his method of Jeet Kune Do.

JET LI is one of the most celebrated martial arts actors of his generation, having starred in numerous films both in his native China and in the United States. These include *Hero, Romeo Must Die, Lethal Weapon 4* and the *Expendables* series.

STEVE McQUEEN was an actor. Popularly known as 'the king of cool', he became one of the biggest stars in Hollywood during the 1960s. At this time Bruce Lee and Steve became close friends and remained so for the rest of Bruce's life. Steve was one of the pallbearers at Bruce's funeral along with James Coburn, Robert Lee, Peter Chin, Dan Inosanto and Taky Kimura.

NORA MIAO is an actor known for appearing in numerous martial arts and romance films in Hong Kong and Taiwan. Nora first met Bruce on location in Thailand during filming of *The Big Boss* and went on to appear alongside him in *Fist of Fury* and *The Way of the Dragon*.

MOZEZ is a singer, songwriter, producer and notable collaborator with the group Zero 7. Born and raised in Jamaica, where Bruce Lee was considered an icon, his first experience of Bruce Lee was watching *Enter the Dragon*. This led to a fascination with his films and eventually his philosophy and writings.

DOUG PALMER is a retired lawyer and was a friend and student of Bruce Lee. After seeing Bruce at a gung fu demonstration in Seattle, Doug was keen to train with him. Doug joined Bruce's gung fu class and the two remained friends, with Bruce inviting Doug to spend a summer with his family in Hong Kong.

RANDALL PARK is an actor, director, producer and writer, who has appeared in numerous films and television shows. Growing up as an Asian American, he looked to Bruce Lee as a cultural icon and role model. In Randall's own work he seeks to humanise his community through comedy and personal experience.

GEORGE TAKEI is an actor, author and activist, possibly best known for his role as Hikaru Sulu, helmsman of the USS Enterprise in the television series *Star Trek*. In 1993, George narrated *Bruce Lee: The Curse of the Dragon*, a documentary about Bruce Lee featuring contributions by Kareem Abdul-Jabbar, Linda Lee Cadwell, Chuck Norris and others.

VAN WILLIAMS was a leading television actor of the 1960s. Best known for his role in the detective series *Bourbon Street Beat* and its sequel, *Surfside 6*, he also starred opposite Bruce Lee in *The Green Hornet*.

TED WONG was a martial artist and teacher. Having studied Jan Fun Gung Fu and Jeet Kune Do under Bruce Lee, he became one of only two people (the other being Dan Inosanto) whom Bruce certified as a teacher of Jeet Kune Do. Ted went on to serve on the boards of the Bruce Lee Foundation and Jeet Kune Do Society until his death in 2010.

In cases where it was not possible to interview contributors, archive text was used from the following sources:

John Benn's quote has been sourced from an archive interview via YouTube.

James Coburn's quotes have been sourced from his interview with bruceleelives.com and archive interviews in which he remembers Bruce Lee via NatterNet.

Jesse Glover's quotes have been extracted from a short film he participated in, *Remembering Bruce: A Tour of Seattle*, and a martial arts press conference.

Grace Ho's quotes have been extracted from her interview with Geraldo Rivera and interviews from the Lee Family Archive.

Taky Kimura's quotes have been sourced from his contribution to the video *Remembering Bruce Lee* with the kind permission of his son, Andrew Kimura.

Brandon Lee's quotes have been sourced from archive interviews via NatterNet.

Joe Lewis's quotes have been sourced from an archive interview in which he recounts his memories of Bruce Lee.

Steve McQueen's quote has been sourced from his eulogy to Bruce Lee.

Van Williams's quotes have been sourced from his contribution to the video *Remembering Bruce Lee* and the Comic Book Central podcast.

Ted Wong's quotes have been sourced from the documentary *Death by Misadventure* (1993).

INDEX

INDEX OF CONTRIBUTORS

LONG RANGE ~

→ REAR HAND SWING
SC 1 ①   SC 2 ②

→ TACKLE SC 4 ①   SC 5

→19A   →20

→ SWING 7 ④   SC 8 ③

→7A   →8A

SWING 10 ①
SC-   SC· 11

SELF-DEFENSE

LONG-RANGE :— *Surprised Attack*

SIDE — ATTACK SA-1   SA-2   SA-3   SA-4

FRONT — REAR KICK SA 8   SA 9   SA 10

REAR

KODAK PLUS X PAN FILM   520

KODAK TRI X PAN   1739

626   LM 3

PARTIALITY
THE RUNNING TO EXTREME

FLUIDITY
THE TWO HALVES OF ONE WHOLE

EMPTINESS
THE FORMLESS FORM

CREATED BY GENESIS PUBLICATIONS